Designing Exhibitions

Second Edition

To Celia, Felix, Lucy and Camilla

Designing Exhibitions

Museums, heritage, trade and world fairs

Second Edition

Giles Velarde

Ashgate

Aldershot • Burlington USA • Singapore • Sydney

Published by

Ashgate Publishing Limited
Gower House
Croft Road
Aldershot
Hants GU11 3HR
England

Ashgate Publishing Company
131 Main Street
Burlington, VT 05401–5600 USA

Ashgate website: http://www.ashgate.com

British Library Cataloguing in Publication Data

Velarde, Giles.
   Designing Exhibitions: Museums, Heritage, Trade and World
   Fairs. – 2nd edn.
   I. Trade shows.
   I. Title.
   659.1'52

Library of Congress Cataloging-in-Publication Data

Velarde, Giles.
   Designing exhibitions: museums, heritage, trade and world
   fairs/Giles Velarde. – 2nd edn.
        p. cm.
   Includes bibliographical references and index.
   ISBN 0–566–08317–5
   1. Trade shows. I. Title.
   T396.5.V45   2001
   659.1'52—dc21   00-54332

ISBN 0 566 08317 5

This book is printed on acid free paper

Typeset in Leawood Book by Wileman Design

Printed in Great Britain by MPG Books Ltd, Bodmin, Cornwall.

Contents

List of illustrations

Foreword

Will the year 2000 be marked for innovative exhibitions and be remembered – rather as 1851 was for the Great Exhibition – as an inspirational year, setting examples for many national and international exhibitions in following decades?

Celebration of the Millennium, together with the availability of Lottery funds in the UK, have produced a climate and expectation for excellent, well-designed and memorable exhibitions. While architectural projects are being welcomed and praised, what of the presentation of the contents of the many new museum buildings, heritage and cultural centres? What of exhibits in the Millennium Dome itself?

Has exhibition design advanced at all since the first edition of this book? Within the last 12 years the working methods and tools of the trade have certainly progressed; the use of computers is now virtually universal, graphic production techniques are extremely sophisticated, audio-visual presentations are at last foolproof, materials and construction methods have improved and manufacturers of lighting equipment now address the specific needs of exhibition designers.

Even the quality of 'the visit' has improved, with queues at popular exhibitions reduced or eliminated by the general introduction of timed ticketing. However perhaps it is too early, at the time of writing, to judge whether design standards are on a general plateau of acceptability or achieving summits of excellence.

Visiting museums, galleries and exhibitions is still a most popular leisure activity. Nevertheless more people than ever are now accessing them via the net. With the possibility of 'touring' a gallery or museum, viewing their complete holdings or visiting an e-exhibition – all without leaving home – the actual experience of the real visit could be under threat. Moreover, perhaps the visit is now seen as only part of an overall experience: desirable but not essential. How will designers react to this? I hope by bringing all their influence to bear on all aspects of this experience.

Design for the presentation of collections is still a basic function of a museum (an area in which I have been working for over 30 years) but political and economic pressures have now altered the emphasis away from design to new management.

Much museum design work is now outsourced. Theoretically this should inject new ideas into what some see has become a rather traditional and staid medium; but designers who do not have the benefit of the received wisdom available to an in-house team are often at a disadvantage, so whatever is written on the subject of exhibitions is to be welcomed.

Giles Velarde has championed exhibition design, initially as a designer but then through writing extensively in the design press; here he has always promoted the principle that reviews of exhibitions should be not just a general discussion of their content but a critique of the whole communication and presentation. In 1988, distilling his wide experience and wisdom, he wrote *Designing Exhibitions*. This new edition will be invaluable, introducing a new generation of aspiring exhibition designers (and a timely reminder to the older generation) to both good practice and pitfalls in the complex and exciting medium of exhibitions.

MARGARET HALL, OBE, RDI

Preface to the First Edition

Exhibitions are at best magic, and at worst dreary trudges around gloomy trade shows or museums. The purveyance of magic is, of course, a serious business. Despite this, most people go to exhibitions in the expectation of having a good time – there is no reason why they should not – but it is easy to design or formalize the pleasure out of an exhibition and end up with something which, while fulfilling the basic requirements, remains a sterile and unprepossessing display. The magic element therefore, after people have been persuaded to go in the first place, is to enlighten and, it is hoped, entertain them at the same time.

It is possible in the generally indoor world of exhibitions to erect wonderful structures with essential facts communicated through marvellous illusions, but these illusions should never dominate the information. The style should never overpower the message, nor the personality of the designer ride rough-shod over the exhibitor.

Exhibiting things is an ancient profession. There is very little difference between the stalls of the money-lenders Jesus found in the temple two thousand years ago and the Business Efficiency Exhibition at Olympia. Moral values may have changed; the construction will certainly be different; but on both occasions the exhibition was there to persuade the public to buy the services on offer. In fact, the basic considerations were identical. The physical constraints were dictated by the place and the characteristics of the people involved, and people were 'selling' to people.

Selling is often seen to be an ugly word, but it is what an exhibition is for. In simple terms, the commercial exhibition stand is designed to sell a product and the museum exhibition is to sell ideas. Both activities make certain basic demands: they must attract visitors, they must hold the visitor's attention and they must inform the visitor. In the first example they must persuade the visitor to buy and in the second to want to know more.

While dividing exhibition production into a number of obvious categories which form the chapter headings of this book, it would also be possible to divide the process laterally under the basic demands mentioned above (to attract, to hold, to inform, to persuade), but this would lead to a complex format and impossibly complicated chapters. It is nevertheless important to remember that the first nail and the last word are all part of the communication process generally described as exhibition design.

No attempt has been made to differentiate between commercial and non-commercial exhibitions, for the author can see no fundamental difference. While many museum exhibitions are permanent, as many are temporary. Though most museum exhibitions are simply informative, they would be useless if no one visited them, stayed for a while, learned something and went away enlightened. They must sell themselves. While many commercial exhibitions are simply for indirect selling, the same criteria apply and a huge number of informative and prestige exhibitions are simply for enlightenment or information. Whether the materials in one exhibition might have to last 20 years and in another 20 days, they are dealing with the same commodities: information, objects, people and space. The commercial and museum fields, therefore, are hopelessly intertwined and, although the museologist might dismiss the Motor Show as trade and the car salesman might regard the museum as fuddy-duddy, they are both actually doing the same thing.

Materials and fittings comprise an area of danger in a book of this kind: it would date very rapidly if exact types of material or fixings were to be quoted constantly. These materials vary and evolve continuously. The norms of 20 years ago and today are completely different, as indeed they will be in 20 years' time. This book, therefore, ignores specific materials as much as possible and attempts to aim at broad principles, descriptions and methods. It is hoped that this book will help the reader in the process of exhibition production, but whereas the first nail has been mentioned as a starting point, there is no attempt to specify the type of nail or where it should be put.

The little sister of exhibition design is display design, often called 'p.o.s.' or point of sale design. In order to clarify the terminology, the word 'display' will be used a great deal. Display is what takes place in an exhibition. There will be many displays in an exhibition and the process of mounting an exhibition is often referred to as 'putting on a display'. But this book does not deal with p.o.s. design in any way, for that is a field exclusive to shops or points of direct sale. You can rarely walk away from a commercial exhibition with an object - only the desire or intent to buy one. There are probably books about p.o.s. design and there are certainly many courses which cover it in art and design colleges. Not so with exhibitions: there are very few books and only one known full-time course on the subject at the time of writing. The problem is that such a wide area of design knowledge is required to design an exhibition successfully that the ideal training is certainly degree level and most probably postgraduate level. This is only very recently on offer in the colleges of the United Kingdom.

All design should be a thoughtful process; to be a good designer is to be an acute observer and understander of people, who can use this observation and understanding to serve certain ends. Design is also the manipulation of style, taste, colour, tone, shape, form and decoration to make something that will perform a function. Many people believe that if an object performs its function well, it will have an intrinsic beauty. 'Form follows function' is the phrase emanating from Bauhaus days which sums this up, and it is hard to look at a satisfactory hand tool, sailing boat or vehicle without seeing the sense in it.

But the function can only be properly fulfilled if the designer has thought about the solution to the problem. If he becomes obsessed with expressions of his own taste and style, and injections of his own personality, the design will fail. It may receive transient acclaim, but it will play no part in the advancement of knowledge and the improvement of life. Exhibitions, no matter how temporary, can be part of that essential progress. If their function is to sell something, then there is nothing wrong with that – unless they fail.

In the process of designing, interaction between the designer and contractors, carpenters, technicians, sales and business people, managers, painters, electricians, bureaucrats and scientists is essential. These interactions are enhanced if the designer keeps a cool head and remembers that all of them are people with problems, pressures, aspirations and dreams, just like him- or herself. It costs nothing to be polite and thoughtful. It will massively benefit the whole process, and therefore, inevitably, the end result.

This book is based on the wide experience of one person, fed by the knowledge and experience of others all along the line; particularly by seven years spent with the exhibition designer and architect Arthur Braven. A great deal is owed to those early days, trotting in and out of contractors' workshops and meeting specialist craftspeople with whom the author has worked very happily over many years, and their names now fill a large address book.

The address book of any exhibition designer is his or her most valuable possession, so it is humbly hoped that this book might find a place somewhere near it.

GILES VELARDE

Preface to the Second Edition

It took about two years to write and produce the first edition of this book. At the end of that time, almost to the day, I left my secure post as head of design at the Geological Museum (now the Earth Sciences wing of the Natural History Museum) and set up in free-lance practice. Having been employed constantly since 1958 it was something of a culture shock, but more importantly it brought me into contact with a whole new set of people and experiences. At the same time the major museums in the country were responding to government changes which affected their entire philosophy with regard to presentation.

Times were changing. Instead of assuming that visitors would automatically come, museums had to make them come, frequently to pay to enter and spend money within the premises. Slowly the senior staff in the museums adapted or were replaced to cope with these new circumstances, but it is dangerous to assume that good museum design started when they went commercial. It did not. In fact some might say that commercial pressures produced worse exhibition design than had existed previously. The closing down of a number of in-house design departments eliminated the possibility of proper research. Quite understandably freelance practices have very little time for research and experimentation; the best place for such work is within a large organization.

In the world of commercial exhibitions very little changed. The computer-driven techniques that were being explored by the more advanced museum, world fair and trade show designers in the 1980s became more and more commonplace and therefore cheaper and more affordable. In fact it is hard to think of a single technique that can be added to those available to designers in the 1980s and, sadly, some of the less electronically oriented ones are in danger of being lost.

Techniques are not what make an exhibition, but the wider the range of techniques available to the designer, the better is the chance of successful communication.

Computers of course now dominate all areas of exhibition design. The design itself, 3D and graphics are now generally entirely executed using computers. Meanwhile computers are used to control revolves, models, animatronics, Pepper's Ghosts, interactive displays of all sorts, lighting and sound, in fact all special effects. But they are only a useful tool; to display in exhibitions simply using computers and screens, something which totally dominated the World Fair in Seville, would seem to me to be a waste of time. The world fair might just as well be put on the Internet and feed a far wider audience.

At the time this second edition is being put together the United Kingdom is going through a period, rather like France a decade ago, of what is called monumental architecture. This is architecture that seems to be designed to commemorate a period of prosperity and national successes. Funded by the National Lottery and private enterprise, great structures are popping up all over the land. Time will judge their excellence or lack of it, but some of these structures are intended to contain exhibitions of one sort or another. It is very clear that some of their architects and probably their commissioners are unaware of the considerable exhibition expertise that exists in the United Kingdom. Some such buildings are indeed designed to try and act as what might be termed interpretative architecture. They cannot; they may be sculpturally fine and thematically styled, but the basic rules of exhibition design must still be possible to apply within them. If they cannot, then the buildings are essentially failures. There is no such thing as monumental exhibition design. Exhibitions are, and always will be, ephemeral. Any exhibition designer who hopes to go down in history immortalized by his constructions should stop reading now and go off and do something else for a living.

This second edition therefore needs a comparatively small amount of change. In the light of further help from my editor as well as the other exhibition experts I have consulted, together with my own experience since the first edition appeared, certain chapters have been added, renamed or amended. If some of the exhibitions illustrated in the original edition now seem a little dated in style, this is not important. At no point does this book attempt to teach style, fashion or taste. It is entirely preoccupied with the essential skills and practicalities of design and the philosophy – if that is not too grand a word – of presentation.

GILES VELARDE

Acknowledgements

I am very grateful to David Varley ARCA for his help in updating The Words chapter. Times have changed somewhat in the management and production fields since the first edition and I am obliged to Nick Fraser of Fraser Randall for his help in the now re-titled The Production chapter. Some new illustrations have been used and I would like to thank Peter Higgins and Shirley Walker of Land Design as well as John Furneaux and Laurie Stewart for access to their photo libraries. I am also grateful to my friend and colleague Adrian Wood for his ready and willing advice on all matters technical during the production of this second edition.

Because of changes that have taken place and the author's own experiences over the past 12 or so years, one new chapter about The Client has been added; The Design chapter in the first edition has been split into The Principles and The Techniques and some chapters have been renamed. The chapter entitled The End Result was originally written by Mick Alt, who was one of the first people to work in the field of evaluation in the UK; since he sadly died the author has updated this, with the assistance of Dr Patricia Sterry of Salford University. Her research over the past years has led to the setting up of a new MA course at Salford provisionally entitled 'Museum, Heritage, Exhibition Design' and aimed at postgraduate students.

In 1980 I wrote a letter to James Woudhuysen, then Editor of *Design* magazine, criticizing the ignorance displayed in the writing of a recent article about exhibition design. A few weeks later I was invited to *Design* to discuss the possibility of more informed articles on the subject, and to my surprise it was suggested that I should write a series of critical pieces about museum exhibitions up and down the country. James Woudhuysen's faith in my ability to do this was touching, and I embarked upon a secondary writing career with ever-increasing pleasure. I have managed to stay in print more or less continuously since that time, and I will always be grateful to him for that start.

In September 1985 I spent a happy few hours showing two Frenchmen around a new exhibition at the Geological Museum in London, explaining some of the complex techniques that had been used to communicate the detailed information. At the end of our time together they pressed me to write a book about exhibitions. I took this as a compliment, but it set me thinking. Completely separately, a month later the Design Council approached me with the suggestion that I submit a proposal for a book, which I did. In the spring of 1986 I went to the Reserve Géologique in Digne, Haute Provence – from where my two visitors had come – and gave a series of lectures. It was these lectures which gave me the basis upon which to build the book. I am therefore most grateful to Guy Martini and Alexandre Maucoronel, the Director and Chief Technician of the Reserve Géologique in Digne, for giving me the confidence and opportunity to gather my thoughts before writing.

I should also like to say that without the help of my wife Celia I would have found even this second edition a considerable struggle. As in all other aspects of my life, she is my indispensable partner.

GILES VELARDE

1 The exhibition

EXHIBITIONS come in all shapes and sizes. As a result they mean many different things to different people. It is not even possible to be too specific about what the term 'exhibition' means, as it is one of those words which have several public meanings and even more 'professional' ones. It is a semantic jungle into which we must advance rapidly, or this book will never get started.

To deal with the public meaning first: it is generally used for exhibitions of paintings or shows, such as the UK Motor Show or the Ideal Home Exhibition.

Nevertheless, it is so much associated in the public mind with paintings that many an exhibition designer has been asked over a gin and tonic if he or she arranges the paintings and the lighting. Surprisingly enough, at the time of writing and despite some conspicuous advances, this is the one area of exhibition design still largely dominated by amateurs.

Exhibitions, shows, displays, **fairs** are all words used to mean the same sort of thing when exhibition professionals communicate with each other. The first exhibitions were probably displays of goods for sale on market stalls. Even in those simple circumstances efforts were, and still are, made to display things in such a way that people are encouraged to move close and admire them. But what are they admiring? The beautifully stacked apples or pears, or the beautiful stacking in a neat, orderly arrangement? Is the stall holder doing it to please himself (or hide the back of the fruit which is rotten) or to attract the buyer? In that peculiar seller–buyer relationship it is undoubtedly done to sell more, and

General view of the Motor Show at the National Exhibition Centre, Birmingham, 1987.

Central feature of the Ideal Home Exhibition, 1987.

the stall holder knows it. So the ancient and effective market stall, now thousands of years old and still going strong, has evolved to the technically sophisticated razzmatazz of the Motor Show and, in the meantime, has spawned **trade fairs**, **world fairs**, **eco-centres**, **heritage centres**, contemporary museum **galleries** and exhibitions, **science centres**, experiences and travelling exhibitions of one sort or another.

The exquisite market stall remains commonplace throughout the world; indeed that type of display can still be found in the marble halls of Harrods in London.

Chinese pavilions at world and trade fairs specialize in arrangements where quantity, and therefore presumed quality, are the only message. But exhibitions have to be separated out from stalls and shops as the former are very rarely associated with direct sales. The whole purpose of an exhibition is to persuade people of the good quality of a product; to make them consider purchasing, rather than actually purchase.

For this reason commercial exhibitions have evolved into high-pressure events, where most of the selling is done by salespeople to salespeople. Wholesalers therefore persuade other wholesalers or retailers to buy and sell on, in possibly another form, to a customer sometimes way down at the end of the line. These exhibitions therefore are often completely removed from an end product. Plastics, for instance, in their crudest form, along with detailed **specifications** of their properties, could be sold to a manufac-

Harrods Food Hall.

turer who might only make part of a product which is passed on to another assembler, who might make the final product to sell to you or me.

Of course as soon as information is brought in beside the product, things start to get complicated. Words take up space; people reading them take up even more space. Pictures and diagrams are needed as part of the explanation. Pictures need space and, if many pictures are required, where will the space come from? Slide shows emerged in the 1960s, so why not have a spoken commentary? So the contemporary exhibition begins to emerge, more and more remote from the eventual customer – except of course in museums or heritage centres. Here the line of communication is direct. In any such display the '**curator**' should be trying to communicate directly with the actual user. There is no inter-mediary here; the basic circumstances are as primitive as the market stall. While museums might fulfil similar purposes, they have to employ much more subtle means to reach so many different types of visitor.

Displaying to sell, delight, persuade and enlighten deals with the same basic commodity: three-dimensional, informative space.

Trade fairs

The illustrations of trade fairs demonstrate exhibitions in the widest possible variety, from the simple **stall** to the **multi-decked**, **island site**, exhibition **stand**. Some background information is therefore required. Trade fairs take place all over the world, all the time. At any given moment there will be at least one trade fair going on somewhere. These are exhibitions established for manufacturers and are frequently categorized. Book fairs, food fairs, motor spares fairs, cycle shows, computer shows, business efficiency exhibitions, museum and heritage services – practically everything has its own trade fair. They are the exhibitions at which the various trades meet to sell components or services to each other, to catch up with the competition, to buy components and, as often as not, to have a good night out with the boys or girls. The public is rarely invited, and barely knows they are going on.

A typical trade fair.

Huge halls exist in major and minor cities of the world. In London we have Olympia and Earls Court and the Business Design Centre. The National Exhibition Centre is near Birmingham. Most of the halls are purpose-built; some are adapted from their original purpose (the Business Design Centre in Islington was formerly an agricultural exhibition hall). Usually the buildings are owned by a local council or a limited company and space inside is let to exhibitors in packages of square feet or metres. These are allocated along predetermined **aisles**.

The usual procedure is for a scheme of **booths**, stalls or stands to be let out on a first come, first served basis. The plan is normally arranged to accommodate a simple structure called a **shell scheme**. This is an empty stall of a consistent size, possibly four metres deep by four wide, with thin board **walls** papered and painted white, an adequate

National Exhibition Centre, Birmingham.

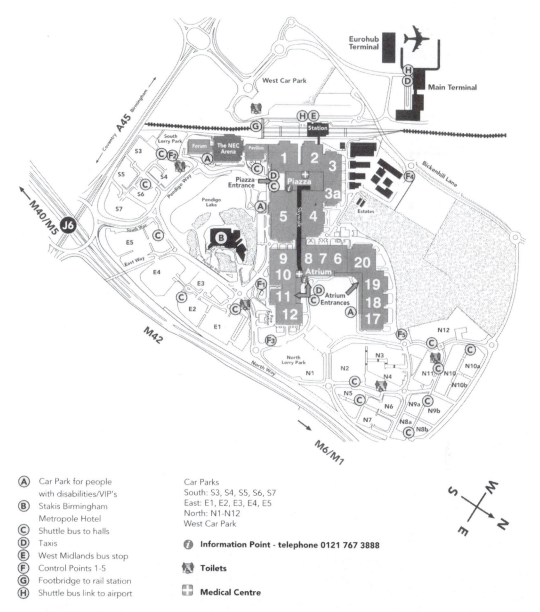

(A) Car Park for people
      with disabilities/VIP's
(B) Stakis Birmingham
      Metropole Hotel
(C) Shuttle bus to halls
(D) Taxis
(E) West Midlands bus stop
(F) Control Points 1-5
(G) Footbridge to rail station
(H) Shuttle bus link to airport

Car Parks
South: S3, S4, S5, S6, S7
East: E1, E2, E3, E4, E5
North: N1-N12
West Car Park

(i) **Information Point - telephone 0121 767 3888**

Toilets

Medical Centre

National Exhibition Centre, Birmingham. Superb communications by rail, motorway and road.

floor covering, sometimes an 80–100 mm **platform**. A board perhaps 400 or 500 mm deep is put across the front of the stall to carry a name, and behind it will be simple, adequate lighting. The walls are suitable for supporting panels or lightweight objects. This very simple box can be hired for the duration of the show and it is quite possible with careful design to turn it into something very attractive. It is also often possible to request the space only from the organizers and to design an exhibition stand oneself. The advantage is that, of course, there is a great deal more control and, provided that the organizers' regulations

Government information stand, National Exhibition Centre, Birmingham. Notice that the people on both these exhibition stands are as important as the displays.

The Business Design Centre, Islington: once an agricultural fair hall.

and the neighbours are respected, a much more dynamic **presentation** can be attempted. The aim of the latter enterprise is to separate distinctly the company or organization from its neighbours, to accommodate special exhibits or displays, and generally to have greater control over the expensive piece of territory which has been rented.

With a greater outlay of money it is generally possible to buy an island site and build an exhibition stand. Again, the rules of the organizers must be accepted, but frequently they allow for the construction of quite exotic structures. **Double-deckers** have an extra floor which doubles the **exhibition space**.

In this kind of enterprise it is not only

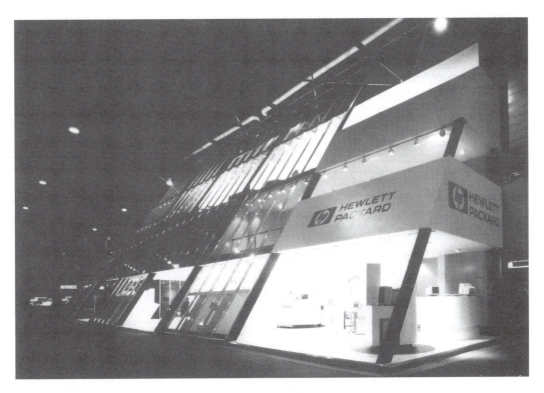

A double-decker by Furneaux Stewart for Hewlett-Packard. By going on to two floors the designers have increased the available floor space from 350 to 854 square metres.

the rules of the organizers that must be considered, but also local or national government regulations concerning safety. Structures which support people over the heads of others must of course be soundly built, **fire-resistant** and offer clear means of escape; but it is still possible under those circumstances to build quite fantastic, effective and graceful structures which will enormously enhance a product and provide a superb showcase for new products or special developments.

It is most important when considering exhibiting within a shell scheme-based trade fair to try and pick a site at the earliest possible moment. There are many factors affecting the selection. A site looking down an aisle is clearly going to be noticed by many more people than a site lost halfway down a raggle-taggle of identical booths. Corner sites and sites facing the entrance to a trade fair are obviously prime positions, as are island sites. An outside corner site naturally has less walls for display, but it commands more aisle. A site below windows on the outer wall of a hall can be poorly positioned, as it is hard to compete with daylight, particularly when the sun is low. The one thing over which there is no control is choice of neighbour but, as soon as this is known, it is as well to get in touch and come to terms over conflicting displays (which could be only a few millimetres apart at the edge of the stand area). Another important factor affecting site selection is the presence of heavy or bulky exhibits; if these are involved it is vital not only to have a site which can accommodate them, but also to have adequate aisles and **headroom** to facilitate lifting machinery. Frequently, **exhibitors** choose their own sites without reference to designers. Of course some exhibitors are experienced pickers, but some are not, and it is as well to involve the designer from the outset to ensure that a thoroughly useable site within the allocated budget is chosen.

World fairs

Many a city with a dynamic Mayor and a go-ahead Chamber of Commerce has considered the possibility of having a world fair. There is in fact an international organization in Paris specifically set up to control the displacement of such fairs around the world. They come in 'classes' which denote size, regularity and characteristics. Those that remain in our memories are generally the Class 1: super-colossal fairs such as Montreal in 1967 or Seville 1992.

The more common are smaller specialized fairs. Small is a relative term, however. The fair in Knoxville in 1982 set out to achieve perhaps half-a-million visitors a month, and actually achieved double that for its six-month summer stint. Knoxville was very successful, so it is perhaps a good example to describe further.

European Community Pavilion, Seville, 1992.

In the late 1970s a dynamic local businessman and member of the Chamber of Commerce decided that the economy of that romantically-named Tennessee town needed a lift. The City Council had, in the middle of the town, a derelict wasteland with all its attendant problems. There was a disused mill and station, a swamp and rubbish tip, all crying out for redevelopment. What better than a world fair to focus attention on Knoxville's charms and facilities, as well as cleaning up the town? The comprehensive and well-drafted proposal for a world-class fair was presented to the World Fair Headquarters in Paris and eventually sanctioned. Invitations were sent out under the theme of 'World

The British Pavilion, Expo '67, Montreal. A persuasive design but critics thought the message a little confusing: the disintegrating Union Jack falling down the factory chimney, perhaps.

US Pavilion, Expo '67, Montreal. Buckminster Fuller's startling contribution to 1960s' architecture.

Energy Resources' (the Tennessee River Authority has its headquarters near Knoxville) and 21 major countries agreed to participate. The parent country, the US, would gain national prestige by building a magnificent pavilion which would remain as a permanent research facility for the University of Knoxville. The European Union submitted a bid for a combined **pavilion** and they, like all the other major countries participating, were allocated space in specially constructed temporary industrial buildings. Australia, Canada, China, Hungary and South Korea were among the other participants. A committee was formed, architects appointed, volunteers co-opted and an administrative office

US Pavilion, Knoxville World Fair, 1982. This pavilion was retained as a research facility for Knoxville University.

established. The derelict site was landscaped and rapidly transformed into a park. The swamp became a lake, the old mill and station were refurbished and added a touch of old-fashioned class to the site. One end of the park was transformed into a funfair with the biggest ferris wheel in the world at that time. Concessions for restaurants, hamburger stalls, novelty shops and boutiques were granted. Eventually the foreign participants arrived, took over the empty sheds and transformed them into air-conditioned palaces of national prestige. Meanwhile a 'sunsphere', containing a revolving restaurant, was jacked 100 feet up a trellis steel column to provide the obligatory landmark invented by Monsieur Eiffel 100 years before. Audiovisual displays and electronic gadgetry abounded; an **IMAX** cinema was constructed to serve the American pavilion and various giant corporations built their own pavilions.

In April 1982 hundreds of pavilion managers, designers, shopkeepers, restaurant managers and fair organizers stood anxiously by their posts as the gates were opened. They need not have worried: the sums had been right. The first visitors swarmed into the pristine park and within a few hours the hosts to the huge crowd knew they had a success on their hands. The timing, the site, the theme, the weather were all perfect. For Britain the 'Falklands factor' was having its effect and large queues grew to visit the British section of the EU pavilion, with the Germans the best of a dull bunch. The very longest queue, standing for three hours in tropical heat, was for the Chinese pavilion; but the Australian pavilion, which had nothing to recommend it but brilliant design, slowly built up enormous popularity. Their formula was exactly right: a simple **story line**, text at the right levels and easy movement inside the pavilion which had two entrances and exits. The whole thing was a triumph of experience applied to good design and management.

What did Knoxville get out of it? Six months of free-spending tourists (a million a month); the fine US pavilion as a boost to the University; a park instead of a derelict site and a huge lift to the economy of the town and region. The commercial exhibitors, the national pavilions and the city benefitted from the international publicity. Suffice it to say that Knoxville considered it well worth their while to embark on the project, and although the New Orleans World Fair two years later was not a commercial success, there seems to be a never-ending cycle of them.

Public trade shows

These exhibitions, usually annual events with massive attendance figures, frequently start with a day or two devoted to the press and trade visitors only. After this they throw their doors open to the paying public. Some, like the Boat Show in London's Earls Court at Christmas, are seasonal events without which the year would not seem quite complete.

The Ideal Home Exhibition in the spring is another very popular exhibition, clogging up the streets of West London for a whole month. The Chelsea Flower Show, regularly attended by the Queen, has the same effect on that part of the city but for a shorter time,

The Boat Show, Earls Court, 1988. The massive and rarely used swimming pool comes into its own once a year.

London's Chelsea Flower Show, 1982. Most people who visit this show are not really aware that they are at an exhibition.

Who is selling what at this Motor Show?

cut flowers being what they are. The Royal Show, a great agricultural exhibition held in a specially designated and facilitated setting at Stoneleigh in Warwickshire, mixes exhibits with competitions, while in the autumn the Motor Show, either at Earls Court or the NEC near Birmingham, is another seasonal landmark. Because of the massive public presence at these shows, the **by-laws** governing stand construction and fireproofing are very strict. This does not hinder the creation of some very exotic structures. At the Boat Show, the normally hidden swimming pool is uncovered and filled with water to provide a suitably aquatic stage in which to float the most eye-catching boats and around which to build an exotic setting, reproducing some far-off resort and harbour. Fashion parades are held on this central feature, while beyond are thousands of square metres of more conventional display space, often sporting yachts and power boats too big to be floated in the pool. Some of the exhibits shown here are among the biggest boats ever seen on dry land; the exhibition is built around them after they have been manoeuvred into the near-empty hall. Apart from this, and its central feature, the Boat Show is fairly conventional. Boats are such compelling exhibits that very little is needed to emphasize their charms. Cars, however, which should come into that category, seem to bring out the greatest excesses in display – as they often do with their drivers – and while it is enormous fun for a male exhibition designer to see pretty, near-naked girls draped over highly polished coupés on press day, it is hard to see what they have to do with cars. (Nothing, though a great deal to do with selling.) This is of course what leads to the phenomenally costly methods of display used in these promotions; mirrored **revolves** and **tilts**, **multi-screen** audiovisual projections, specially made **cutaways**, **animated models** and so on. It is easy to deride these lavish expenditures, but out of them comes real trade and just occasionally a development of real value to exhibition designers in other areas of the profession.

Science centres, heritage and eco-centres

In the early 1960s, Philips Industries at Eindhoven decided to celebrate their then prime position in lighting and communications **electronics** by building a permanent exhibition explaining the field of technology to the ordinary Dutchman in the street. They built what was for that time a fantastic mushroom of a building and employed the English designer, the late James Gardner, to design the exhibition itself. It is justly and internationally famous to this day. Ahead of its time, it became a model and guide for the building of establishments such as the Ontario Science Centre in Toronto and the Exploratorium in San Francisco. Meanwhile throughout the western world the conservation lobby has made us more and more aware of the importance and value of our surroundings. Information centres with permanent or semi-permanent exhibitions are being built in or near areas of historical or scientific interest to remind us of their importance, to explain their value and often to raise money to preserve them. Where these are built in a town or village they are generally called heritage centres, and in rural surroundings they are often called eco- or ecology centres.

Heritage centres usually consist of a building which is preserved in its own right with the exhibition built into it. Displays and **tableaux** of life in and around the village or town, artefacts, documents, old film and photographs are woven into displays, large and small. Obviously the generally ancient or elderly buildings in which these displays are housed

have to be respected; building an exhibition inside an exhibit is no mean task. Frequently the work is undertaken in conjunction with a specialist architect. It is as well if the designer and the architect are brought together from the start, and not at the last moment long after important decisions about lighting, power supply, ventilation and access should have been taken. Eco-centres specialize in presenting the country-side to the interested visitor. Near the Camargue in the South of France, for example, is the famous Musée Camarguais, the work of a team of designers inspired by Georges Henri de la Rivière, essentially devoted to explaining man's involvement with the region. Deep in the heart of the Camargue itself is the Réserve Nationale du Camargue, devoted entirely to explaining the natural history and wildlife of the area. The public is given a varied presentation in

Ontario Science Centre, Toronto, now serves as a guide to state and national organizations embarking on ventures of this kind.

Part of Evoluon, the Philips permanent exhibition at Eindhoven in The Netherlands, designed by James Gardner in 1966.

The Camargue Museum in the south of France. The old sheep fold is now a fine regional museum. This interior view shows the museum's original use.

a modern exhibition, the centrepiece of which is a television camera permanently monitoring the life of birds in a nest. There is a lecture theatre and facilities for school parties. A hundred miles away, up in the mountains of Haute Provence at Digne, there is a **geological reserve** where a fine exhibition explains the geology of the dramatic scenery and its effect upon the flora and fauna. The design, construction and installation of these displays is all exhibition work, and can be a real challenge to the designers involved.

Museums

The line between contemporary science as described in the last paragraph and historical information is so thin in some museums as to be invisible. Museums in the public mind,

The British Museum. Along with its massive permanent collections, its own design team has produced an enthralling sequence of temporary and permanent exhibitions, which started with the Tutankhamun Exhibition in 1972.

however, are generally associated with the past. Since the late 1960s the word 'museum' has lost its old-fashioned connotation. 'Museum piece' is no longer the derogatory term it used to be. One of the first major exhibitions to take place in a museum was 'Britain Can Make It' in London's Victoria and Albert Museum (which itself grew out of the Great Exhibition of 1851), designed by James Gardner in 1946.

This was a milestone in exhibition design and helped to put the profession on the map. While a few distinguished exhibitions took place in museums in the UK after that, it was not until the Tutankhamun Exhibition, designed by Margaret Hall and opened in the British Museum in 1972, that the British public really caught hold of the idea that museums could be places of fun.

Shortly after that, in the same year, 'The Story of the Earth', which was a permanent exhibition in the Geological Museum (now the Earth Sciences wing of

The Sport and Leisure section of the 'Britain Can Make It' Exhibition in 1946, designed by James Gardner with Basil Spence and Robert Gordon.

the Natural History Museum) – again designed by James Gardner – opened and the public realized that even exhibitions of natural science could be exciting and interesting.

It was always taken for granted that the Science Museum would be fun, since there were so many interactive displays there; but until that time it had not been considered possible that the public could interact with an exhibition about geology. These major developments sparked off a rebirth of museum interest. Designers were called in, where previously curators and draughtspeople had cobbled together displays. In London's Natural History Museum, for example, an entire department – the Department of Public Services – was set up to formulate a policy for interpreting natural sciences to the public. Designers and technicians began to be employed on a permanent basis in national and provincial museums. Across the Atlantic, in Canada and the US, similar developments were taking place. There an early emphasis was on exhibit evaluation. Commercial marketing and psychological experiments were done in an attempt to find out exactly how much people learned from exhibits. In the Milwaukee Museum, extensive research programmes were set up under Professor Chan Screven of the University Psychology Department, and several papers have emerged from that source on exhibit evaluation before production, during an exhibition, and after it is over.

James Gardner's 'Story of the Earth' exhibition at London's Geological Museum, 1972.

The Great Exhibition of 1851: not the first major exhibition in the world but very much the beginning of what might be described as the modern type of popular exhibition.

The 'Skylon' central feature of the Festival of Britain in 1951.

So museums are now places for exhibitions: some permanent, often referred to as galleries; some temporary. Permanent constructions of course demand higher standards of both content and construction than temporary exhibitions, but both frequently deal with precious or irreplaceable objects so the difference need not be too great. Higher standards of content are necessary quite simply because it will receive far greater scrutiny than a temporary structure. An immortalized mistake can be pretty hard to live with. The reason for higher standards of construction is evident. Both sorts of museum exhibition, as indeed that in the following paragraph, may require security and **conservation** to be taken into account. There is a comprehensive work, *The Manual of Curatorship* (Thompson, 1984), as well as experts on both these subjects which the ignorant (and that includes the author) are advised to consult when the need arises.

Exhibition of photographs at the Hayward Gallery, London, 1984. Fine exhibits but not hung with any consideration for effective communication with the visitor.

Art galleries

As previously mentioned, this is the one area of exhibition design dominated by the amateur. In national galleries, there is a body of curatorial expertise which still dictates the placement of pictures in an exhibition. The word '**interpretation**' is unfamiliar to most amateurs in the exhibition context, and the effective movement of people through space is not even a consideration. Provincial art galleries such as the Laing Art Gallery in Newcastle and quite a few others are far more adventurous as interpreters of fine art. Clearly, if the exhibition of paintings is on a theme, this will emanate from the curator, but when considerations of planning, labelling, lighting and general display are dominated by non-designers it will be to the detriment of the exhibition. Sadly, this often goes unremarked by the press who visit the exhibition on preview day under exclusive and less crowded circumstances than the public, who have never been led to expect anything better. In fact, badly- or non-designed exhibitions of paintings are commonplace. The public will put up with horrendous conditions: overcrowded galleries, bottlenecks and **voids**. These are generally accompanied by terse, badly positioned **labels** in too-small **typefaces**, demanding a to-and-fro movement between the pictures' viewing distance and the labels' reading distance, sometimes up to 10 metres. At the time of writing, designers, when used in most national art galleries, seem to be employed simply to decorate. It is hoped that one day they will be allowed to design.

Experiences

The word '**experience**' has arrived on the exhibition scene only in the past dozen years. It is a word used to describe any kind of public event or happening for which no other word exists. All experiences have to be contrived. They vary from animated reconstructions of historic events or battles to the experience cobbled together by the New

One of the cars used for taking visitors around Jorvik, York: the first of the experiences.

A mobile exhibition. All the visible structure can be dismantled easily and placed inside the lorry for transit.

Millennium Experience Company for the Millennium Dome. These happenings require sometimes a huge variety of skills. The important thing about them is that they should be conceived, planned and tested before they are started. It was very clear that the building for the Dome was conceived before its use had been at all clearly defined.

The best team to put together an experience would be led by an established entrepreneur with some knowledge of informing and moving people, information and objects in three-dimensional space; they should be supported by exhibition designers, architects, quantity surveyors, engineers and marketing experts. Between them they should be able to plan something housed in an appropriate building in the right place, at the right time, at the right cost. Then it might be successful from the outset. No matter what the Dome achieved over the year for which it was conceived, it is abundantly clear that it got off to a very bad start.

Within all these broad types of exhibition circumstances there are some important categories, mostly associated with practical considerations.

Travelling exhibitions

These are exhibitions which actually travel, with wheels or keels: caravans, vans, trains, ships. Even a fishing boat has been used by the Canadians. Its holds were exhibition space,

The *Cutty Sark* in dry dock at Greenwich, London, contains an exhibition about its life and times and is itself an exhibit.

A showcase construction system, Inca, by Click Systems Limited.

Disney World, Florida. It may seem corny here but people can play a very valuable role, even in informative displays.

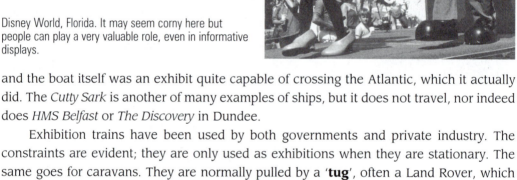

and the boat itself was an exhibit quite capable of crossing the Atlantic, which it actually did. The *Cutty Sark* is another of many examples of ships, but it does not travel, nor indeed does *HMS Belfast* or *The Discovery* in Dundee.

Exhibition trains have been used by both governments and private industry. The constraints are evident; they are only used as exhibitions when they are stationary. The same goes for caravans. They are normally pulled by a '**tug**', often a Land Rover, which also carries a generator to supply power where there is no access to mains. Again, the constraints are obvious but it is amazing how much information can be condensed into the close viewing conditions of a train or caravan section. One most important factor is maintenance but, clearly, for a travelling exhibition it is a peculiar problem, generally demanding a permanent driver and maintenance staff.

Another difficulty is siting. With a train, ship or caravan, suitable **venues** must be found and arranged well in advance, for it is no good embarking on a travelling show until a schedule of **sites** and visits has been arranged.

Portable exhibitions

These of course do travel as well, but only to be erected and dismantled again and again. There are many manufactured **systems** available for building temporary exhibitions, most

Part of Jorvik, York. Smells are used in the various parts of this ride-through exhibition.

of which are exactly suitable for such treatment. They also generally come in especially-designed boxes or crates, so to adapt a design to suit them makes a great deal of sense. Exhibition systems will be dealt with at greater length in Chapter 6, but of course they are not the only solution.

It is often essential or beneficial to design one's own portable exhibition. Important considerations are weight, size, packaging, precious objects, ease of erection, durability in the hands of many different users and clear instructions. Also, of course, exhibitions with a **working**, moving or audiovisual content must be carefully considered and rejected if **maintenance** and power cannot be guaranteed.

There are many other types of exhibition venue: **conferences**, hotel, library or station foyers, special '**one-off**' exhibitions like the Festival of Britain in 1951 or Ulster '71,

Part of the National Motor Museum, Beaulieu, Hampshire. No real effort to display stylishly has been made here, probably because the objects have such powerful attraction in their own right.

the 1984 Garden Festival in Liverpool and its offspring, and of course the Millennium Dome. There are '**information-only**' exhibitions, set up by government bodies or research stations at trade fairs, to explain laws, policies or scientific developments associated with the trade in question, or government-financed services available to the exhibitors. There are **open days** such as those at the Transport Research Laboratory, or the Building Research Station; exhibitions in libraries or learned societies; exhibitions that verge on Disney World such as Jorvik, the Viking exhibition in York where there is a ride by electric cars to take the visitors around the exhibition at a controlled pace; and the National Motor Museum at Beaulieu in the New Forest, England.

There are completely new museums, devoted to a single theme or one hitherto undisplayed industry. Zoos too are becoming more and more attuned to using interpretative exhibitions as a part of the service offered to the public.

All these should involve exhibition design, as they are all dealing with objects and information in space as areas of learning, fun and enlightenment.

2 The designer

DESIGNERS, like exhibitions, come in all shapes and sizes. 'Designer' is itself an odd word. Unlike the term architect, which always denotes a designer of buildings, the term designer has always to be qualified – in this case with the word 'exhibition' – and we have already seen that a great number of people are not sure what an exhibition is. This is probably why, in the early 1960s – when art colleges shook themselves out of the complacent and class-conscious distinction between fine art and commercial art and into the multidisciplinary establishments they are now – exhibition design was left out. In the smaller, diploma-oriented colleges, display courses proliferated; but now there is at least one course in the UK offering an honours degree in museum and exhibition design, and the Masters course at Salford University in Heritage Exhibition Design Studies.

Where do exhibition designers come from? In the writer's own early experience, they were mostly 'lapsed' architects. However, the first designer really to earn a reputation for

A visual for a trade fair stand for the Piano Manufacturers' Association, 1974.

exhibitions was James Gardner, and his background was certainly not architectural. Gardner first came to public attention with 'Britain Can Make It' in 1946, but a leading involvement with the Festival of Britain in 1951 put him firmly on the exhibition map, along with other designers like Misha Black, and architects of the time such as Hugh Casson, Basil Spence and Arthur Braven. Today's generation of exhibition designers comes either from the one university course or second-hand, as it were, generally via **graphics**, architecture or 3D design. None of the last three is adequate. The first deals with flat presentation of information and the last two with people and space. Even in colleges which have fine reputations in both graphics and 3D or media, it is commonplace for the courses to be totally separated when it comes to projects concerning exhibitions whereas, as will be seen, it would be an ideal area in which to develop interdisciplinary skills and group or team activity. The truth of the matter is that a feel for, and an almost sculptural comprehension of, space is essential to the exhibition designer, as is a feel for graphics and the flat presentation of information. It is quite possible with experience for architects, graphics or 3D students to develop the understanding required and, when they do, they should specialize in exhibition work.

As some have now realized, exhibition design across the wide range from trade fairs to museums and heritage should be taught to degree and post graduate level, as a discipline in its own right. Selling is such a vital function in the western economy that the need for this should be evident. Since 1970 museums have become an integral part of our educational system and, just as there are no unqualified teachers, museum exhibition designers should be equally well trained. While there are now some university courses, it might be hoped that the potential client will respect the fact that an enormous variety of skills are needed. Despite the need for specific exhibition design training, it is also true that the exhibition designer is a jack of all trades. So many factors go into making exhibitions at their best that, without the broadest possible knowledge of methods of presenting information, the designer can be lost for solutions to some of the complex communication problems that emerge.

What qualities are needed to create the creature? They come in two categories: first, personal qualities; and second, professional qualities that result from training or experience.

Personal qualities

It is interesting that the standards of design in museums in the 1980s should have been so high, for despite some obvious exceptions these standards actually fell in commercial ventures, which in turn seem to have declined since their heyday in the 1960s. Meanwhile, a swift glance over the profession as it stands today shows practitioners coming from all fields of design or, in the author's case, art college. This is only a bad thing if the design work is done not by a regular practitioner, but – as happens so often – by someone wholly ignorant of it, when it is possibly delegated by senior partners in design firms to junior assistants as 'a bit of fun'. Of course, exhibition design is a serious business.

Understanding three-dimensional space

This means the ability to think in the round, to see a flat plan and to be able to project it mentally outwards into three dimensions; to be able to explore spaces in the mind; to place objects in space and to walk around or through them. Training in sculpture, interior design and architecture helps to develop these facilities.

Understanding people

The designer needs to have a sensitivity to people and how they behave, interact or respond to various physical circumstances; how they enter a room, how they react to artefacts, diagrams, photographs and even each other. Every designer should be at least in part a psychologist; in the peculiarly intimate relationship between displays and people it is essential.

Understanding structure

While it is not essential to have a degree or diploma in engineering or structural design, a certain amount of common sense about it is vital. When necessary, structural expertise can be easily brought in, but it is important in the early planning stages to know that ceilings do not generally float in space unaided, floors actually have to support enormous loads, and walls will fall down if they are not propped up. Moreover, most inanimate things on legs will fall over sideways if they are not stiffly braced. This is all pretty basic information, but amazingly silly proposals have had to be rejected by the organizers of exhibitions and their experts.

Theatrical flair

Exhibition design is considered by many to be very close to theatre. Clearly here the audience is static, and captive, and its basic reason is entertainment. However, more and more exhibitions are being built with entertainment in mind, such as Jorvik and Beaulieu in the United Kingdom, the Powerhouse in Sydney, and the Exploratorium in San Francisco. Many recent plays have been written with the accent on information (*Mary after the Queen* for instance), as indeed was much of Shakespeare and before him the Mystery Plays.

A sense of theatre is a valuable attribute for the successful exhibition designer as well as the ability to see the drama in a subject and to exploit it to attract a bigger audience, or explain complex ideas in an enthralling manner.

Is this a play or an exhibition? Real artefacts, true story, real actors! 'Mary After the Queen' by the Royal Shakespeare Company, Stratford-upon-Avon.

Solving problems

Others, particularly Edward de Bono, have written on the subject of lateral thinking. As far as this book is concerned, it is the ability to open the mind to all kinds of solutions to design problems unconstrained by conventional attitudes. Take, for example, projection of images on to **screens**. Is it just that simple? Practically everything can be the object of projection: smoke, spray, gauze, water, milk, people, floors, leaves. This is lateral thinking, and of course it can be applied to countless other circumstances. The ability to solve problems by this expansion of thinking is invaluable.

Intelligent interest

There are two classic areas where it is most difficult to design effectively and objectively. The first is where the designer is not interested in the subject, and the second is when he is too interested, or is even a specialist. In the first instance it is obvious that if the designer is not all that excited, he or she is going to find it very hard to persuade anyone else to take an interest. In the second instance, if the designer is a near-specialist he or she will neither communicate objectively nor be able to interpret the subject in a jargon-free manner. An intelligent interest is naturally essential. An exhibition designer should be the sort of person who is well informed, well read and able to take a short-term intense interest in any subject. In this way he or she can act as an effective interpreter, guiding the specialist suppliers of the information towards a comprehensible presentation. If the designer can understand the client's explanation, it is likely that his or her interpretation will be understood by the visitor. This leads naturally to an interest in communication and interpretation.

Communicating

It helps if the exhibition designer is literate and enjoys communicating. There is a body of opinion which thinks that the best exhibition designer is an extrovert 'exhibitionist', not just having an interest in communication but needing to communicate, almost to show off. Perhaps this body is right; there is certainly very little point in embarking on a career in exhibition design if you are shy, withdrawn and do not like to mix! However, the communication must be explicit, brief and effectively levelled and balanced.

Professional qualities

These are qualities which become more evident after receiving specialist training or experience; some may lead naturally to a career in exhibition design but none of them constitutes specific training for such a career.

Interior design

This is training in the comprehension and use of interior space, which is quite different from exterior space; if it is to be related effectively to exhibition design it should be training to place people, objects and information within a specific empty space. It entails the comprehension of that void, its characteristics and potential, allied to a broad grounding in safety factors and the law relating to the safety of visitors with regard to fire, structure and services.

Structural engineering

Naturally, any structure that will contain people, or support or house heavy or precious exhibits, must be safe. Basic training in this area is vital and consultation is essential before any final design solution is reached.

Graphics
It is possible to communicate without words, but they are normally an important ingredient. Chapter 5 is devoted to words in exhibitions, the understanding of which is fundamental training for a designer. There is no need for professional, degree-standard qualifications, but the exhibition designer must appreciate the necessity for the use of a professional graphic designer in almost any successful communication exercise.

The English language
Training in clear, precise writing is essential. First, for any professional the ability to communicate concisely is of enormous help in pitching for work or drafting reports, synopses and **briefs**. Second, as has already been stated, communication is what exhibitions are about and, while exhibitions of words alone are anathema, exhibitions of objects must be supported at least minimally by words. Frequently the designer will take on the role of scriptwriter for want of anyone better to perform the function; this is just acceptable on a small temporary display, but on anything of any substance professional writers should be used.

Lighting
This is a great deal less haphazard than it used to be, and actual training in lights and lighting techniques is invaluable. In museums light can be a major problem due to its effects on fragile fabrics, artwork and dyes. Conservators should be on hand or consulted. Meanwhile, there have been many new light fittings and techniques developed over the years and it is as well to be up to date.

Drawing
Drawing board skills and drawing ability were once obvious practical necessities. Nowadays the computer has become as valuable a tool as the pencil was when it was first developed. However, while the computer is a magic device, drawing and sketching from life are marvellous ways of perceiving and understanding people, objects and space. Any designer will be improved by regular activity of this kind.

Photography
The same is true of photography. Many photographic techniques are exploited in exhibition work. Photographs and photographic enlargements are frequently used; slides, photomontages, films and television are all photography. Such techniques are also used in the production and enlargement of text and diagrams. A basic grounding in photographic techniques is essential.

Model making
Models are frequently used for presentation of designs to a client, or in the exhibition itself. An ability to make presentation models is of value, though it is a time-consuming

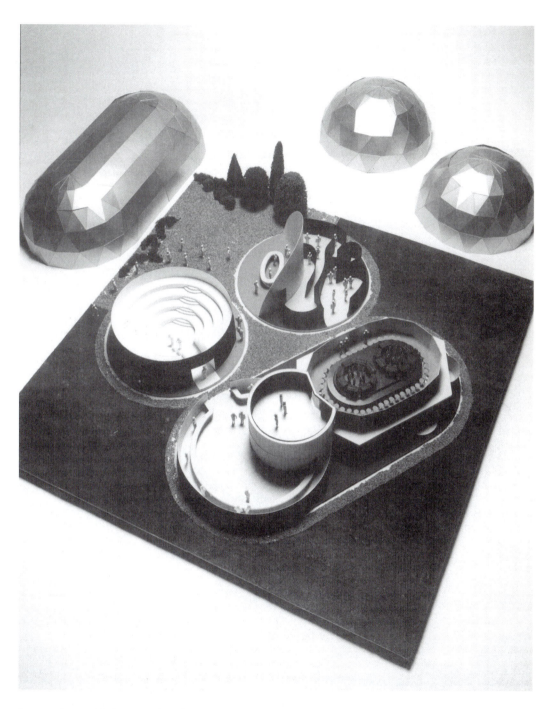

Presentation models for the Fit for Life touring exhibition, 1988. Models are powerful alternatives to visuals, but sometimes too powerful if the client discovers that the eventual product is not exactly like the original proposal.

Aluminium fountain outside Sea and Ships Pavilion, Festival of Britain, 1951. Water can be exciting both visually and aurally in an exhibition but a nightmare if it goes wrong.

process. This ability leads to a greater understanding of the problems involved in the making of models for display purposes when working with professional model makers.

Water and plumbing

It is surprising how often water is used in exhibitions, sometimes as a decorative feature, fountain or cascade, or as a necessary part of an exhibit. Some idea of water's quirks and peculiarities is essential, as is a healthy and wary respect for it. Water out of control is, of course, something to be avoided.

Electronics and mechanical engineering

Not everybody can acquire electronics or **mechanical engineering** skills. The author, for example, has little ability with regard to anything technical. However, regular up-dating, observation and an understanding of the potentials of contemporary technology are, along with an inventive mind, of great benefit in devising the often complex three-dimensional means of communicating things simply.

Computers

Clearly these play a huge part in all sorts of communication and design. Anything written about them now will be out of date almost before the fingers leave the keyboard. An early introduction to computers is now normal in most educational circumstances and it is therefore vital, as is regular contact with their development.

A computer *circa* 1966.

A laptop computer of ten million times the capacity, 1999. Photo by Adrian Wood.

Painting

Murals and mural treatments are often used in exhibitions. It is necessary to acquire knowledge of their production, **reproduction** and enlargement. Professional mural artists should always be used, and they can be found through their professional associations.

Illustration and diagrams

Again, these are frequently used. Clearly, it is better to use professionals, as with painting, but it is important to have some training in illustrating and in generating attractive and informative diagrams out of often complex information in order to understand the problems which can arise.

Mural, transparencies and objects in 'The Story of the Earth', Geological Museum, 1972.

Management

Chapter 9 is devoted to this subject, from which it should become clear how vital good **management** is to good design. At best, designers should be supported by management services, but at the very least a designer should know how to manage the production of an exhibition and to control the finances involved.

Advertising

This is generally associated with claims for a product. Exhibitions generally demonstrate the product itself, and that is their great value: an inbuilt integrity. When an exhibition stand is erected simply to make unsubstantiated claims, this is advertising and the author has no expertise in the field.

Although many people have gained their knowledge of these things by experience, they are ideals in any training programme and there is no reason why they should not be part of a three-year degree course. The diversity and range of subjects which make an ideal background for the exhibition designer is therefore very broad and high-lights the 'Jack of all trades' aspect. However, with the right training it should be possible to be master of at least one: exhibition design.

An advertisement you might or might not believe.

3 The client

NOW that there is at least one degree course in museum and exhibition design in the United Kingdom and other postgraduate activities are in hand, then inevitably the focus of attention should be turned on the training of the client. The experience of the author has led him to the vain and the modest, the clever and the foolish; to those who are both clever *and* stupid and, of course, to the informed and sensitive. Designers too can vary from awful to brilliant; however they are not necessarily potted plants that need nursing with care lest they explode with rage or walk off in a huff.

This chapter is about the client, but it is worth remembering the qualities that were described in the previous chapter about the designer.

Project definition

Clients should define the problem they want to be solved before selecting the designer. Paradoxically it is often the case that the client, untrained in these matters, cannot define the problem; therefore a designer is needed before the client realizes it. The client may be able to describe the problem in simple terms – an exhibition in such a place about so and so, a new gallery in this museum using that collection – but there is a plethora of aspects to the problem that such simple desires do not describe. Chapter 12 will, among other things, look into formative evaluation: that is the assessment of whether such a solution will satisfy such a demand, but even before that a decision has to be made about the actual need for an exhibition in the first place. Some subjects are hopelessly unsuited to exhibition. Concepts (ideas) for instance generally make very poor exhibition subjects. Some evolutionary circumstances, well described by scientists, will make a far better **animated film** than they will an exhibition. Government information, statistics, the results of research, all make pretty dull display material. The best person to advise on this subject, and indeed on the suitability of various spaces or architectural designs for such spaces, is either an experienced exhibition designer or a company that specializes in the definition and analysis of museum and exhibition design projects and proposals.

Computer terminals in 'Treasures of the Earth', Geological Museum, 1985. Both this and the next picture demonstrate how radically these two types of display have affected the thinking behind exhibition design.

Feasibility studies

Before starting this chapter it seemed a good idea to look into other publications for guidance on the subject. Sadly none of the books about exhibitions or museums that were consulted contain the phrase '**feasibility study**' in their indexes. Turning to the dictionary however was more profitable: 'an investigation to determine whether a particular project or system is desirable or practicable'. What could be more succinct or accurate than that?

Unfortunately over the past years, particularly in the museum profession, such studies have earned a poor reputation; perhaps this is because some of them have proved to be inaccurate – or indeed too accurate. It is probably as wounding to spend quite a large sum of money on a study that recommends that you do not continue with your project as it is if the study turns out to be wrong. However, it is clearly wise before embarking on a major project to do some testing of the waters. The ideal team to conduct a feasibility study might consist of a management expert, a surveyor if new or repaired old buildings are involved, an architect, a quantity surveyor, a museum, heritage or commercial exhibition expert and an exhibition designer.

Hands-on displays, the Discovery Centre in Glasgow.

Concepts and design studies

Part of the study might consist of a **concept study** – designed to test a concept. It usually consists of a number of sketches of the proposed concept and a simple set of choices. This is then tested by taking it around the neighbourhood of the proposed project or to people who are considered likely to use the completed enterprise. The idea is to get their reaction to it. It is a highly professional business (see Chapter 12), usually conducted under the aegis of marketing experts, using field workers armed with a set list of questions.

A design study comes later in the day. The feasibility study has proved positive, the concept has been modified as a result of the survey that has taken place; a design proposal is produced. The design study consists of drawings and **visuals**, sometimes with a model, to ensure that the client is completely apprised of what is proposed and therefore happy to continue with the work produced by the architects, designers and quantity surveyors ideally working in concert with each other.

The dangers of moving into major projects without such testing can be considerable. In the initial stages of the planning for the British Pavilion at the World's Fair in Seville in 1992, all the architects who were asked to pitch for the work were invited to bring an exhi-

British Pavilion in Seville, 1992.

bition designer into their team. None of them did so. When the eventual designs were considered none of the assessors was an exhibition designer. What was eventually described by the architectural press as a fine piece of architecture turned out to be hopelessly unsuited to its purpose: display. This went unnoticed by most of the architectural critics of the day. The building ended up with a massive **audio-visual** (A/V) show in an expensively darkened space and three or four small gondolas of the sort one might find in an airport terminal.

Together with project management consultancies, there are sufficient established exhibition design practices around these days for the client to buy in some expertise, on a non-committed basis, to assist in the early stages of project definition and development. If during those stages the client discovers that he has a considerable rapport with the designer, then ways should be found to keep that designer on board for the whole project.

If the client finds the designer useful but does not feel that they will work well together on the actual project, then they can part company at this early stage without rancour. But at least the eventual designer is likely to be presented with a well defined project, a clear brief and, with luck, a suitable site or piece of architecture in which to place an exhibition.

Finding designers

The most important thing about the client should be that he or she is able to bring out not only the best of the designer, but the best of the entire client–design team. The ideal client will know how to find the right designer. Having done this at the right stage, the client will use the designer to the full, commanding the best not by bombast and dictation, but by enjoying and sharing the creative process that produces great design. Exhibitions are ephemeral; they do not therefore invite the same social or cultural standing as the more permanent or definitive creations of product designers and architects. Nevertheless they are very important. Exhibitions play a massive part in the economy of any country and, on another note, they might frequently constitute the only vehicle that can bring great designs, past and present, to the attention of the public.

The process of finding a designer is as often embarked upon with great trepidation as it is with blind arrogance. The client should never be looking for someone simply to execute his own creative or entrepreneurial ideas – for those purposes a **draughtsperson** is needed – nor should the client be frightened that employing a designer will remove the project from his or her control or add significantly to the costs. The whole point of using a designer is to bring a creative professional mind to bear on a particular problem – in this case an exhibition. The client–designer relationship, like all human relationships, is crucial to a good result, so the finding of a designer depends on two things: first, the selection of a designer whose work the client respects, and second, the selection of a compatible personality as the project will almost inevitably turn into a fairly stressful production period.

The sad fact is that, despite the proliferation of media and museum studies courses around our universities and of design management courses in the design colleges, very few people are taught how to be a client. This may seem stupid – what, after all, is a client? We are all clients at one stage or another, of a plumber, a lawyer or a cleaner. So how do you train a client?

Client training

There is, of course, no such thing as a school for clients or a degree in the subject, so with great trepidation this chapter will take the first tentative steps into what will probably turn out to be a minefield.

What are the qualities required of perfect clients? Firstly they must recognize their need for assistance; this involves the same kind of humility with which we go to the doctor or dentist, the former at times of need, the latter (in the case of the author) in times of desperation, which is best avoided. The client must approach the designer knowing that help is available and with a willingness to place themselves in the designer's hands. The second requirement is trust. Moving away from medical analogies, trust also involves various parameters for which the client is responsible. These are described in Chapter 4, but it is important that financial limitations are clear and explained at the outset for they can be the cause of great tensions and even, if care is not taken, litigation. So far therefore we have *need*, *trust* and *cost*.

More intimately, however, *rapport* is important, for the creative process is one of action and interaction. If there is no personal chemistry, no delight in the sharing of ideas or the solving of problems, no respect for the other's creativity, intelligence or knowledge, then there will be no pleasure in the project and no really satisfactory solution.

Another vital element is *access*; this works both ways. The client must at all times be available for the designer and, likewise, the designer must always be available for that client. It is no good if the smartest and most relaxed person on the design team's staff pitches for work and the client never sees him or her again. Similarly if the client delegates the responsibility of the production, he must do that wholeheartedly, making the junior to whom he delegates not only a part of the designer selection process but also the actual client. If the original client turns up on site at the last minute and finds the whole project not to his liking, then he or she only has themselves to blame.

Finally we come to basic *knowledge*. Many non-designers think that a designer is someone who designs everything and anything; others think that an architect is the only real sort of designer and all the rest are fashion designers or interior decorators. The fact that design, rather like surgery, is a profession within which there are many specializations is a completely strange concept to many non-designers. The result of this is that many a potential client needing an exhibition to be designed goes firstly to an architect. The architect, eager for a project and possibly one that looks easier, more profitable and more fun than usual, snatches at the chance and embarks on building an exhibition. Some large multi-discipline design practices without proper exhibition design expertise do the same. The end results, and there are many examples, evince the kind of errors and failings that the professional exhibition designer will avoid as a matter of course.

Most of the qualities described above can be put in such simple terms that one would imagine that they should be learnt not at college but at the knees of one's parents. After all, they boil down to the basic necessities of community life: need, trust, financial common sense, getting on with people, consideration for others and being there for others when they need you. What is surprising is how these basic human attributes, common to most of us, fly out of the window when confronted by the comparatively unimportant circumstance of producing an exhibition.

Selecting a designer

There has been much discussion in design circles and in the design press over the past few years about the ethics involved in design selection. After much experience and after working with many other design practices, the author is able to describe a typical design selection process that is both unfair for the client to impose and unethical for the designer to accept.

Such a circumstance is likely to be conducted in the following way. First, the potential client assembles a list of designers from sources such as the Design Council, the Design Business Association, the Chartered Society of Designers, the *Museums Yearbook* or a National or Area Museum service. They write to everyone on this list asking for CVs, resumés or brochures. They make a short list from these submissions, frequently not informing those who have not been selected. They put together half a dozen packages which they consider describe the proposed project and send them to the short-listed designers or design practices. They ask them to present themselves at eleven fifteen on the umpteenth, bearing with them their proposal for the solution to their problem. What they are in fact asking for is very many hours of free creative work for which they, the client, pay nothing and then make a generally pretty ill-informed choice.

So why is this unfair and unethical? First, this type of client is either too lazy or too overworked to do the necessary research involved in finding the right designer for the right project. Second, the client, who is presented with five or six free solutions to his problem, might feel that he has got himself a very good deal and can pick and mix from these solutions, practically getting the job done free of charge and possibly with the aid of a junior or inexperienced draughtsperson. Third, a designer or design practice keen for work in order to maintain a large staff will submit designs, and the more desperate or unscrupulous the practice, the more time will have been spent on such a submission. So at one extreme it is more likely that such design practices will get the work in the face of competition from designers who rightly refuse to participate in such practices. At the other extreme, the one man band with no work and time on his hands will put in a stunning submission and get a job that he is unable to carry through.

How then should a designer be selected?

There is, of course, a great deal of sense in getting lists from design or exhibition associated organizations; but before this, it is far more sensible for the client to become acquainted with the whole business of exhibition design and production so that any selection process can be both informed and ethical.

A large organization embarking upon commissioning an exhibition designer

should have or appoint a person specifically experienced in such matters: an Exhibition Officer. The responsibility of selection and then the supervision of production should be delegated to this person. In a small organization, a provincial museum, or a company deciding to exhibit for the first time, the director or manager should research the field. They should visit the type of exhibition in which they propose to exhibit, looking at the stands that attract attention and are crowded with interested customers. The curator of a small museum should visit other museums which have similar artefacts or have solved similar problems, and find the ones that seem to reflect similar ambitions.

One of the best methods of selecting a designer is to research the field and interview a number of designers in what is called a **credentials pitch**. This is a meeting in which a designer or design practice shows examples of their work and explains their process of design and production. It is unpaid. After this the interviewer should make a short-list and invite a few designers to enter a paid competition. If a reasonable fee is offered and a proper brief is distributed, then very few designers will turn down the opportunity to visit the potential client and submit their ideas in the form of sketches and documentation at a further interview. If rejected, the cost of production of the ideas will have been covered and, if not, the successful designer will get the job.

In the case of the public company or small business, it is completely up to its principals how they choose the right designer. There are no government, local government or European directives that dictate a selection process. In the case of public bodies, however, there are considerable constraints on both the advertising and selection of designers and architects. One of the bad things about these restrictions is that they generally demand or imply that architectural practices should take the lead. As has been pointed out earlier, however, it is best if the primary involvement is with an experienced exhibition designer. They do not have to lead the project but, if an architect is commissioned without reference to exhibition design, it is almost inevitable that the client (and the designer) will end up with a building or space that is pretty difficult to fill with a decent exhibition.

At this point it would be wise to give more consideration to the qualities described earlier in this chapter: need, trust, cost, rapport, access and knowledge.

Need
There are areas in all our lives when we need expertise that is quite beyond our own capabilities. Medicine has already been mentioned but electricians, television engineers, pest controllers and surveyors come into that category, and we select and accept them usually on recommendation and after research. Exhibition designers should and, to the well informed, do come into that category. At the simplest end of the scale – a small booth in a minor trade fair, for instance – it is dangerous to assume that an exhibition can be put together simply by a commercial representative or the managing director. It is hoped that the skills described in this book will lead the client to realize that even on a tiny scale a professional eye is better than an amateur one.

Trust

Just as we are forced by our ignorance to put ourselves in the hands of some of the special-ists mentioned above, and indeed to trust them, so it should be with an exhibition designer. If the selection has been done wisely, the client should be forming a connection with someone who is equally keen on forming a good relationship. Time and experience have shown that someone trusted is far more likely to perform to their maximum ability than someone who is regarded with suspicion. Clearly the client must keep an eye on development, and the competent designer will have arranged meetings at various stages to ensure that the client knows and is happy with what is going on. No matter what, trust is essential: if it is absent from the client–designer relationship, then quite frankly there is very little point in maintaining it.

Cost

Money is a funny thing, prone to bring out the worst in all human relationships. As will be seen from the next chapter, cost is a fundamental part of the brief, but the brief often comes a little later on in the client–designer relationship – and often with the assistance of the designer. Cost therefore should be discussed openly and from the outset. If a potential client contacts a designer and simply wants an exploratory visit, then if both are local to each other no cost should be involved; if, however, a company or museum in John O'Groats wants the same of a designer in Land's End, then it would be only fair for the company to offer to cover the designer's expenses. If the designer has another client in John O'Groats then it would be only fair for the designer to suggest an exploratory meeting could take place on his next visit to his existing client – good sense and common decency must come into it. If the client is using the designer to help him advance sensibly into the project, then this should be done on a day rate plus expenses. The best way of doing this – at first approach – is to explain the day rate and allow the client to decide whether he can afford it or not; everybody therefore knows where they stand from the outset.

Once the preliminary work has been done, (this is known in France as the **pre-project**) then a fee structure should be agreed, based on percentages of the total cost of producing the exhibition. On a major project, the fee should include project management and graphics, at around 22 per cent. On a small project, just the one designer, graphic design and management included, the fee might be 15–20 per cent. If the designer has been instrumental in the setting of the budget for the whole project, then he will know better what percentage is likely to yield sufficient legitimate profit.

During the stage meetings mentioned under the previous heading, costs should inevitably be monitored by the client, and the designer should be more than willing to highlight expenditure. If peculiar or unforeseen circumstances have arisen and a contingency sum needs to be raised, then this also should be pointed out at the earliest possible stage.

Rapport

Rapport is quite simply personal chemistry; if it is not there to start with it can of course develop. If it shows no sign of developing, working together is quite possible but less fun and probably less effective. If there is instant rapport, watch out – it can occasionally go sour! The client–designer relationship, particularly where the client is fulfilling a life-long dream, can be quite emotional. Both parties should therefore tread carefully.

Access

There is nothing worse than an invisible client or an invisible designer. Clearly in the selection process on a major project it is impossible for the whole eventual design team to be on parade, so it is completely normal for the principal of a design practice to be closely involved in pitching for work. It is also completely normal for that principal to have many other projects on the go at the same time. The client, too, is likely to have other major managerial responsibilities and therefore may be partly represented by a senior manager or director who also will be unable to bring along all the likely associates that will eventually be involved. But one thing is crucial: that there should be decision makers, present at these earliest meetings who will stay with the project. These decision makers, partners, associates or staff members must be involved in the selection and pitching processes, and should be given every encouragement to work together. The principals on both sides must be kept informed of progress, and again a structure should be set up to facilitate this. There are management techniques and books that can be consulted about such things. However, access – that is the ready ability to contact the right person at the right time – must be planned into the project development. Holidays, other project deadlines, contingencies, pregnancies and emergencies should all be recognized as possible and allowed for.

Knowledge

Here now we have come full circle. We know there are courses for exhibition designers. But where is the potential client to gain the necessary knowledge to be an effective client? An effective client is not simply a person who bends to the will of a megalomaniac designer; he or she is someone who attains the project they first described, better than they ever could have hoped for, on time, within budget and to the rapturous acclaim of the public and their peers.

The logical place to look for client training is in design management and museum studies courses. Client training, insofar as it relates to the commissioning of exhibitions, would seem to the author to be of such importance as to warrant more than just an occasional lecture in a one- or three-year programme of studies. The title Exhibition Officer has been mentioned earlier; in any large enough organization such a post, with the necessary staff, should be absolutely normal. Exhibitions place very high demands on all those involved, especially permanent exhibitions. The whole business of accumulating collections, artefacts, samples or products is immensely demanding, dependent as it is on many other people's deadlines and schedules, conservation and value. Working to a strict deadline is satisfying and exhilarating but also very demanding. Pulling deliveries, space bookings, personnel, **contractors**, sub-contractors and finances all together at the right time is an onerous responsibility and not a task to be treated lightly. Such training should also equip the student who ends up in a very small organization, be it commercially- or museologically-oriented.

At one seminar at the Museums Association Conference, none of the participants who had been or were on museums studies courses had learned a thing about such matters. The author's own personal experience has see-sawed regularly between the two extremes: on the one hand is the pleasure of working with a client who is well informed and a delightful companion in the tricky jungle of exhibition production; on the other hand there is the rank idiot who may be academically clever but is too stupid and self-centred ever to be allowed to be involved in the production of an exhibition that serves the public or its specific audience satisfactorily. It has to be remembered that once the designer has left the project and handed over the exhibition, museum, gallery or heritage centre to the client, there is nothing further that the designer can do. If the client decides to shift all the objects, stick labels with adhesive tape on to the carefully considered graphics, buy some unsightly furniture or huge jungle of flowers, or ignore any advice the designer may have offered with regard to the ongoing maintenance and use of the displays, there is nothing the designer can do other than go home and tear their hair out or kick the cat.

Architects

It might seem from this chapter that the author has been taking an occasional sideswipe at architects. This is undeniable but perhaps needs to be clarified. The author is the son of a respected architect and, over the past years, working with architects and understanding the field has often been a real pleasure. On the other hand, there have been times when one has had to work despite them. It is widely recognized that some architects are a law unto themselves; that their clients are so intimidated by their professional and public standing that they are allowed to get away with murder. Architects are designers of buildings – that is their training. It is possibly among the more thorough of all educations given to designers, and does indeed encompass visual understanding and acuity together with certain academic or specialist areas not touched upon in most other design studies. However, the one thing they do not seem to be taught is that their buildings should function in the purpose for which they are designed. It goes without saying that their buildings should not leak, fall down, blow over or endanger anyone's lives. Yet museum buildings, like hospitals, libraries and public toilets, have a specific and clearly defined purpose for which there are a number of works setting out criteria. On many occasions these criteria are ignored while the architect charges ahead producing buildings that he or she thinks will work. They often do not. Some architects create excellent furniture and interior

The Royal Armouries Museum in Leeds.

The River and Rowing Museum in Henley-on-Thames.

design. But only those who devote their whole working life to exhibitions make good exhibition designers. Exhibitions are about communicating with and in three-dimensional space, indoors or out. In a recent architectural publication, exhibition design was described as a 'mysterious sub-set of interior design', a ridiculous and ignorant description. The same article went on to encourage architects to undertake exhibition work during slack periods because it was fun, undemanding and well paid.

The exhibition designer who is asked to construct a building should invite an architect to join his team. The architect who is invited to design a showcase, an exhibition, a hall for trade fairs, a museum, heritage centre or world fair pavilion should ask an exhibition designer to do the same.

What is really sad is that in recent years a number of so-called 'landmark' buildings have been constructed, designed by architects but without any recourse to museum designers. This results in something perhaps very pleasant to look at, but hopeless as museum space: poor circulation, inaccessible and badly arranged mechanical and electrical facilities, too much daylight in some places and architect-dominated displays which struggle to involve the public from any interpretative point of view. The Royal Armouries Museum in Leeds is such a building, and another, the River and Rowing Museum in Henley-on-Thames has gone on to win prizes, both as a building and as a museum.

4 The brief

NOW that we have established what an exhibition is and what sort of designer is required, we are ready to move on to a project. An exhibition will only be built because it has been agreed that it is the only solution to a particular problem; in other words it is the best method of exposition and communication in particular circumstances. It is not possible, or better, to make a film, television programme or commercial. An advertisement, brochure or book is not what is needed. A record will not do. An exhibition is required because there is something to exhibit and a story to be told that can best be put across in three-dimensional terms.

Six things must first be established:

- The aims and exact goals of the exhibition.
- The venue and exact site.
- The information in general terms.
- The objects to be displayed.
- The opening date.
- The budget.

These six factors are basic. If any of them are changed during planning, design or construction the project will be radically affected. It is therefore vital that these factors are agreed between client, designer and management at the earliest possible moment and maintained as crucial to the success of the venture. These six prime factors are described in more detail below.

The aims

Until recently the actual effects of an exhibition were either guessed at or optimistically forecast. Over the last half-century, starting in America, studies have been made to elicit the precise effects of displays using psychological techniques and statistics. These methods of evaluation are

A possession or an acquisition worth parading: the Portland Vase, one of many treasures at the British Museum.

discussed in Chapter 12, but clearly some knowledge of the effect of various types of display is of great value when deciding what one is aiming to achieve. Like all professional expertise, evaluation has to be paid for. This kind of information can affect radically the success or failure of either a commercial or public exhibition; so if there is an insufficient body of experience to help decide the aims, this is probably worth buying in.

These aims can be summarized in the following set of objectives:

- *To sell*: not often in the sense of directly selling an object, but to sell in the abstract – showing an object off for close scrutiny and even handling, so that a client may be persuaded to buy in bulk; supplying a piece of equipment; selling an invention.
- *To persuade*: in the sense of pressuring the public; convincing the visitor that, for instance, 'Britain is Best' or that dealing with agriculture or the environment is best done this way or that. Persuading encompasses respecting the countryside, visiting a certain town, holding a conference here or there, using certain services, voting for a certain party, supporting a cause or visiting a museum.
- *To expose*: by putting a collection on display, giving the public a sight of rare artefacts or masterpieces, getting public reaction to a prototype or architectural scheme.
- *To parade*: a new acquisition or gift; to be seen.
- *To inform*: by describing a new product or concept, keeping the public up to date with commercial, political or social developments.
- *To explain*: new or ancient aspects of science, technology or research and make clear any services available.
- *To advise*: the public about their rights and the law.
- *To generate interest*: in a subject by developing it thematically or systematically.
- *To delight*: and why not? The exhibition can be there simply in order to give pleasure, to entertain or perhaps to allow people an opportunity to see something rare or special.
- *To enlighten*: a mixture of the last four, and what exhibi-

To enlighten: a multi-media display, 'The Story of the Earth', Geological Museum, 1972. This was the first of its kind, dealing with geology, anywhere in the world.

tions are really all about. One dictionary definition of enlightenment is 'to become wiser through knowledge', and the exhibition is a unique vehicle for that.

The site

Without information about the specific site within the venue it is impossible to design. Working in a vacuum is not feasible for a designer, though he can introduce ideas about design philosophy, methods and treatments. Until the site is decided, nothing concrete can emerge. Where is the venue? Variations can be astonishing and great fun, from a barn in the middle of a river delta (the Musée Camarguais) to a car park under a road bridge in central London (the Museum of the Moving Image); from a library in Thurso, Scotland, to a sophisticated, purpose-built complex in Frankfurt. There is no limit to where an exhibition can be, as long as both the exhibitor and the public can reach it relatively easily. The best venue, either on or off the beaten track, has good public transport, parking, restaurant, toilet and power facilities, but some very successful exhibitions make do with a good deal less. Many a 'one-off' show does not fit into the normal run of exhibitions and therefore cannot be included in a trade fair, for instance, at a specifically designed exhibition complex. Special situations are needed for these; so is lateral thinking.

What is actually required is a clean, generally covered space with easy access to power – usually electricity. Examples are station forecourts, hotel foyers, underground or overground car parks, airport terminals, squares, parks, piazzas and city centres. The latter open areas can take tents, **geodesic** structures, **inflatable** pavilions or portable **industrial sheds**, most of which are available for hire. A mobile exhibition may be under consideration; it should be situated if possible near power and easy public access, but again the possibilities are great. Trains, lorries, buses, trailers, caravans, liners, warships, fishing boats and probably even aeroplanes (were the subject apposite and the plane available). Once the decision of venue is taken, the site – the actual specific area within the venue on which the exhibition will be placed – is the next vital piece of information. Ideally a visit should be made to the site by the exhibitor and the designer, and a number of factors noted as detailed below.

Accessibility
Access both for the visitor and the exhibitor: lifts, loading size and weight, lorry or goods access, parking, delivery, unloading and loading gear or platforms.

The size
The length, width and shape of the floor and floor loading.

Height
Overhead obstructions, exposed wiring, lighting or dangerously exposed services, head-

room for cranes or fork-lifts. The ceiling construction and strength; the facility for hanging signs or structures. Anything on the site such as power outlets to which other exhibitors might need access.

Daylight

Is there daylight at all? Will it interfere with display lighting? Will there be awkward oblique light in the early evening? Can it be controlled, shuttered or blinded off?

Services

Electricity, gas, water, drainage, compressed air, ventilation and air conditioning, telephone – where are they all? How easy is it to get to them? What is the electricity supply, phase and voltage (AC or DC)? What is the maximum loading?

The law

The law pertaining to the site if there is general public access is often different if the access becomes restricted. What types of exhibits or displays may be used? Will flammable plastics, timber or fabrics be permitted? Can working exhibits be displayed? Can tall structures be built? What are the fire and safety regulations? If the designer recognizes, seeks out and observes the law – which is generally designed for the good of the public – then there will be no costly and embarrassing changes to make while the exhibitor is trying to entertain his first visitor.

The information

At the earliest possible stage all the information to be communicated must be available, ideally as part of the brief. It does not need to have been edited into perfect exhibition form or text, but it must be there. It must consist of all the ideas that need to be expressed, all the background data and statistics, hopefully everything that a sizeable percentage of the visitors will learn. If it is not possible to get all the detailed data together, many a brief has evolved with the exhibitor knowing generally what needs to be communicated, and leaning heavily on the designer for how to say it.

Some concepts cannot be expressed in the three-dimensional terms used at their best in an exhibition, and the designer's experience will be invaluable in making certain decisions. In organizations that employ their own designers, it is ideal for briefs to be evolved between the initiators of the information and the presenters of the information. In this way no time is wasted in going down blind alleys towards exhibitions which will prove impractical, impossible or vastly expensive. No matter what, it is difficult to start developing any exhibition until a large amount is known about the informative content. There are specialist exhibition editors or **scriptwriters**, and if there is a fair amount of information to be expressed, rather than just simple labels for exhibits, it is at this stage that these professionals should be brought in. Some large design practices employ such people on their staff; a few designers can and do perform this editorial role. In many national museums editors are, quite rightly, an integral part of the design team, while some large companies employ **copywriters**.

The objects

Some exhibitions have no objects except those made in an effort to communicate: special models which 'diagrammatically' explain subjects too complex for either words or illustrations. Ideally, however, exhibitions are about things – to see, hear, touch, smell or even taste. Sometimes they are inside the object on display: the Smokey Mountains; the *Cutty Sark*. Generally, however, they are the vehicles for displaying and some things must be ascertained by the designer at an early stage because, of course, they will affect his or her thinking and planning.

The number and size of the exhibits is clearly important; their point loading too, for a car may weigh a tonne but the load on each of its wheels will be many tonnes per square centimetre. This is the way floor loading is measured. Are the exhibits spontaneously flammable? Fragile? Precious? Will they be sensitive to light, heat or movement? Do they need a special atmosphere or through-draught of air? Do they need a dust-free environment? Do they collect static electricity and dust? Can they be touched? If to be hung on a wall, do they require special hanging points, plinths or barriers? Do they need their own showcases or frames, or will these have to be made? They might be valuable, very valuable or priceless. However, there is no point in hiring expensive security guards before the priceless objects arrive. What are the insurance characteristics in transit or on display? Government property is rarely insured; it is covered by government **indemnity** which simply means that the government will replace it. This is difficult if we are talking about a Turner and easy if we are talking about a tank.

These questions are almost endless, but essential. Other considerations are security, supervision, freighting across borders and through customs, and delivery addresses. A good production manager will take care of the details, but most of these facts must be known by the designer at an early stage because they will affect either the design or other things which could delay or confuse completion and construction.

When all the exhibits have been

An exhibit in the Smokey Mountains National Park, Tennessee. This house is maintained doorless and empty throughout the year.

decided and all their characteristics are known, the designer might make card shapes or models to scale to represent them, and displace them about the site or showcase. Whatever the choice, they must be designed 'in' and not simply left to be 'artistic arrangements' made when they arrive the day before the exhibition opens. This is not a good time to make creative decisions. The designer should be involved in the selection of exhibits where there is a choice, and should see and measure them before they become 'lost' in the lengthy process of packing and shipping. Photographs can help the designer if there is no access to the exhibits and even as an *aide-mémoire* if there is. It is poor practice when the designer is forced to produce a design based on only a skimpy knowledge of the objects to be displayed, and a client who does not provide maximum access to this information cannot blame the designer for a poor display on opening day.

The opening date

This is another vital bit of information required in the brief. It is not actually essential to know the exact day, but it is a good idea to commit all involved to a date at the earliest possible stage. This is particularly important when VIPs are to be invited to open the exhibition. Most trade fairs have a set opening date, determined by the complex calendar for the exhibition hall. These dates have to take into account the building and dismantling times which vary, for instance, between the pre-constructed booth exhibitions of the USA and the Motor Show where huge and complicated stands need perhaps ten days on site to build. An exhibition in a museum or gallery may be tied to an anniversary or a gap in the museum's programme of events.

The suitability of a date must be considered. Obviously a flower show in mid-winter may hit a snag or two, but some dates have problems which are not so obvious. Avoid arranging an opening date which coincides with an important local football match. Beware, too, of special feast-days or anniversaries. Before deciding a date, it is as well to consult the local council and police to be sure that it does not conflict. If it is to be a grand occasion, royalty needs at least six months' advance notice, and sometimes a year.

Some dates are bad for other reasons. Most people write off the season over Christmas and the New Year; ten days are generally lost, so it is fine to open an exhibition early in the New Year as long as an extra fortnight is allowed for preparation. The same is true of summer holidays and, to some extent, Easter. All this applies to Western countries only, and the Middle and Far East have a different set of constraints.

Some days are better than others. Tuesday is a good day – the preceding weekend can be used to cram in extra work and Monday to purchase anything discovered missing on Sunday. But again, these characteristics vary from country to country. Friday is a bad day in the UK. People are prone to want to go home, 'exhausted' by their week's work, so it is difficult to get visitors for an opening celebration in the afternoon. Perhaps it is better in the morning!

No matter their other charms, royalty do galvanize activity to meeting opening dates, and frequently provide the impetus for improving the facilities in an old museum or exhibition hall.

The press must be allowed early access, if you invite them at all, so that an article with a photograph can be produced on opening day. Rumour has it that the press will not come unless there is plenty of drink about, and the phrase 'cordially invited' is supposed to imply that there will be.

So, opening dates have to be picked early and carefully, and not changed. It is useful to have a common goal; besides, if royalty is invited the date really is fixed. A royal visit not only provides an air of excitement, but a stimulus to local councils and ministries to rectify local omissions such as bad pavements outside halls or museums, or bad toilet facilities inside state- or council-owned premises that are to be visited.

However, not everything can be catered for, and natural disasters, assassinations or wars have been known to leave carefully planned openings looking like the Stock Exchange on a Sunday.

The budget

This is the final essential piece of information. A proper **budget** can only be allocated with experience, and any costing quoted here would date rapidly and vary from country to country. The best way of allocating monies is by the square metre or square foot (the former is almost exactly ten times the latter). These measurements refer to a **square metre 'super'**, that is from the floor of the site to the top of the exhibition structure. They refer also to the whole area of the exhibition, public, staff and display space. Obviously a square metre of aisle will cost a great deal less than a square metre of complex three-dimensional display, but an overall costing will serve as a good guide.

Early 'guesstimating' can only be done with experience, but there are a number of known factors that can be ascertained: hire of exhibition space, site rental, square metre cost of graphic reproduction and design, certain special models, hire of furniture, designer's and consultant's fees and so on. Any established designer or exhibition manager should be able to quote approximate costs per square metre for the specific types of exhibitions described in Chapter 1.

As mentioned in Chapter 3, experienced exhibition designers can be found in the UK through the Museum and Exhibition Design Group (a specialist group within the Museums Association), the Chartered Society of Designers, The Design Business Association and the Design Council. Experienced production managers are harder to track down, but the Design Council will usually help with advice.

The cost is an integral part of the design brief. It is fundamental. Designers who exceed their budget by more than 10 per cent (a safe contingency to allow for seasonal price fluctuations and so on) are as guilty of bad practice as those who design an exhibition the wrong way round.

It is important to remember that design, management and consultancy fees should be factored in at the outset.

With the six vital statistics established and agreed in writing, it is possible to embark upon the project confidently, without the fear of radical changes being made which might confuse or affect the design to the detriment of the finished product.

5 The words

ONE might expect in a book about design that when the subject is words it is their appearance – their typography, **layout** and display – that will be discussed. Quite right; but not only their appearance: in order for words to be effective in the 'walk-about' context of exhibitions, it goes without saying that they should be well displayed, but for that to happen the words should actually be composed with display in mind.

Interpretation is the term increasingly used in the context of museum exhibitions and environment or heritage centres. For the lay person it means the interpretation of artefacts, works of art, science and our environment, along with the landscape or local archaeology. In these areas the designer can play an important role. He or she is a lay person when it comes to actual academic study of the sciences involved. The designer's position between the academic source of information and the visitor is of immense value, provided that integrity as a non-specialist is maintained. The moment the designer becomes a fan, a devotee or an amateur 'student', his or her value begins to be lost. As a skilled amateur student, the scientific jargon would become second nature, coupled with an inability to differentiate between the technical language of the academic and the jargon-free explanation which the interested lay person can understand.

A primary, interpretative role, as with language interpreters, should be performed by someone who is fluent in both technical and exhibition languages. A secondary role is more subtle. Before an exhibition can be embarked upon, the designer must know and understand what it is about. To this end the specialist, whether environmentalist, archaeologist, art historian or engineer, must explain the subject and theme satisfactorily to the designer. This process will undoubtedly involve the use of words and expressions that the designer does not understand. In the further explanation of these phrases, an easily understandable version is likely to emerge. If the designer can understand it, so will the visitor. The latter, however, is not a single unified creature of median intelligence, so hierarchies have to be introduced wherein each person can find a level of understanding and so gain something from the information imparted.

It is vital in the academic–designer interchanges for notes to be taken, for academics who are trained to communicate clearly with other academics can frequently communicate orally far more simply and effectively face to face with an interested lay inquisitor. This secondary interpretative role of the designer is much underrated but can, under sympathetic circumstances, eliminate the need for an actual interpreter or editor on a production team.

The arch-exponents of words for simple, eye-catching display are popular newspapers. The editor does not put SEX–DRUGS–WAR in huge print at the top of page one

Is this designed for short-sighted readers?

Why is labelling so often too small?

because the readers are short-sighted; those words are there to be seen from miles away so that the person without the newspaper will buy one, the editor having calculated that those words will attract readers. The choice of headline is a vital part of the sale of news-papers, and the editor can do (and generally does) whatever he wants after that. In very crude terms, this sums up writing for exhibitions. Without giving a dissertation on writing English, it is necessary to dwell for a while upon writing for exhibitions.

The story

This must primarily be a story suitable for an exhibition. It must be strongly visual and factual since concepts, theories and philosophies do not translate easily into three-dimen-sional presentations. The story must be broken down into short aspects, chapters or state-ments, and it must itself be short. Concentrating on long narratives is difficult in the normal standing position of the visitor. Preceding the ideal story must be a title; this too must be short, because it has to be displayed in big print and seen from long distances. This is one of the reasons why companies with long names give themselves distinctive, initials-only logos. The company name is often the first thing to be seen at a commercial exhibition. Special exhibitions in museums or galleries for instance need pithy, easy to say (and remember) titles, and must be graphically satisfactory. Quotation marks, apostrophes and hyphens are untidy in the often huge scale of **fascias**. Some groups of letters, especially upper and lower case together, can create an ugly or even subliminally suggestive shape which is best avoided.

Headings

Assuming that the story can be broken up, the next things to be considered are the titles to these divisions: the headings. These comprise the guide to the lateral subdivisions of the story – and lateral is the word. Information in exhibitions is transmitted and received laterally; the visitor moves around on the horizontal plane. The story is presented on panels or in areas of explanatory text and pictures, or in areas or rooms within the overall informative space. Again, the headings should be short and easily comprehended. They must also serve as a lateral guide and, when read consecutively, present a **synopsis** of the subject.

Hierarchies

Mention of headings and even sub-headings leads naturally to a discussion of hierarchies. Headings are frequently the first level in a two- or three-**tier** hierarchy of information.

Hierarchies are used to enable visitors to dip, with a facility peculiar to exhibitions, into whatever part of the exhibition that interests them. Thus, standing perhaps at the entrance of an exhibition boldly entitled *ENGLISH CHEESE*, visitors from Somerset can read at a glance a summary of everything immediately relevant and then, by a simple turn of the head, can select the section on *CHEDDAR*, a particular interest.

They can then make straight for it, passing Cheshire, Stilton, Wensleydale and so on and, on arrival at Cheddar, will perhaps be confronted by a vertical hierarchy. This is a placement of information in short paragraphs, pictures and examples which can be 'read' downwards to the point where interest expires or technical jargon overtakes the visitors' knowledge. If interest increases with the information being learned, they might be encouraged to move in closer to more detailed displays, so that a mass of hitherto concealed information becomes apparent. Visitors looking at the lowest, deepest level of the hierarchy could almost be 'studying', but they are doing this of their own volition.

If thoughtfully designed, the finer levels of the hierarchy would be invisible to any visitor approaching the chosen section, only becoming apparent on delving deeper and deeper into the subject. This is because another, less motivated visitor might be put off, for example, from going into the Cheddar area at all if a mass of complex and detailed information is immediately evident. Obviously if this vertical local narrative is written in an unbroken way, then it will be difficult to display and therefore read in the way described above; so it must be written in short sentences and

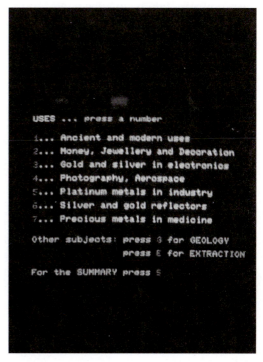

Computer-generated text.

paragraphs, starting, for instance, with the most remarkable or explainable characteristics. This clearly requires experience of exhibitions but, if successfully done, the exhibition and graphic designers will be able to proceed with presentation without having to ask the initiators of the information to rewrite large chunks to suit display techniques.

It is now commonplace for some levels of a hierarchy to be contained in a computer; how precisely this is done will continue to evolve, but it is now so simple and inexpensive that computers – and indeed the Internet – are becoming an integral part of many exhibitions.

One-level exhibitions are of course another completely acceptable alternative; here the producers select a level of intelligence and write all the text with that specific group in mind. There are varying types of IQ: reading, creative and mathematical, for instance, and there are clear differences between the reading ages of 'popular' and 'quality' press readers. Data is available, but in the UK the reading ages vary from between 9 and 17. If, for example, an age group of between 14 and 16 is selected, then it is likely that the content will be easily understood by quite a wide audience; most people in the West attempt at least to reach that scholastic level. There are two main disadvantages to this one-level approach. The first is that these academic levels are only theoretical and thus inexact, and the second is that one level excludes two distinct groups – those well below (young children) and those well above (serious students of the subject or amateur specialists). The hierarchic system at best caters for all, but it demands a great deal more from the producers, writers and designers, and is therefore unpopular with organizations which want a quick production line for permanent exhibitions or a large number of popular temporaries.

Style

Another aspect of exhibition writing which applies right across the board is more concerned with the descriptive style. Colourful, subjectively descriptive prose is both useless and offensive when the object is already there on display. Captions describing 'this beautiful painting' or 'this elegant dress' are simply irritating. The visitor, confronted by the objects, should make an independent decision about beauty or elegance. In effect, the exhibition itself is a superlative factor. The object will certainly not be on display if it is one of several million, or a banal example, unless of course its popularity and ordinariness are the interesting factors. The exhibition must tacitly provide the opportunity for *adjectives* and *adverbs*; all the visitor needs are objects and facts.

Labels and captions

Facts lead us clearly into the area of labels and captions. For the sake of this work, a **label** contains the vital statistics of the object on display, and a **caption** is a small piece of text linking the object to the display around it. The former is therefore informative; the latter

'British Fossils', Geological Museum, 1980. Both object and label clearly legible at the same distance.

descriptive. On occasions, both labels and captions are used by exhibitors to sneak more story into the exhibition, and this should be resisted. The most important thing to be remembered by the writers of labels and captions is that they must inevitably be studied at the same viewing distance as the object to which they refer.

To have to look at one from 5 m and the other from 50 cm is clearly absurd, but try telling that to the average curator in a public art gallery, where the visitors are conditioned by habit into walking three times the distance actually needed. This readability will of course govern the number of words, so we are back to the writing again. Labels must be short and precise, and written in the same way. A picture label might perhaps contain the

The Clore Gallery, London, 1987. Poor relationship between object and caption, the viewing distance of the former being probably four metres and the latter just over one metre.

title, the artist, the **medium**, the date, the size and the catalogue or collection number. If the next label starts with the size and ends with the title, there will be no order for visitors to follow subconsciously. Irritated and confused, they will probably go home.

The copy

To many students and potential exhibition designers reading this book, the thought of actually having to write or edit anything will be anathema. It is essential to say that no designer should have to write any copy for exhibitions; a professional copywriter should be employed wherever possible. The ideal production team for a **narrative** or informative exhibition of any sort should contain, along with the three-dimensional designer, a graphic designer, a copywriter and a manager. In fact, despite the list of qualities considered essential for an exhibition designer, it should be remembered that these are only qualities and cannot replace professional qualifications. Any exhibition designer who does not employ or work with a graphic designer is always going to be operating below par, and any graphic designer who takes on three-dimensional exhibition work without either training or extensive team experience in the subject will be similarly disadvantaged.

Graphic design is an important and complex discipline, but even within its complexity designers are usually not specifically educated in graphic design for exhibitions. While the author is not a graphic designer, and this book is not about graphic design, there are certain basic principles which will emerge from a discussion of the actual design of words in an exhibition.

Presentation

The most important fact to remember is that an exhibition is not a formalized method of informing. There is no such thing as a normal exhibition format, as there is with a book. A book has a clearly defined front and back, beginning and end. Its pages open on a certain side, the introduction will be at the beginning and the index at the end. Page one will always be on the right-hand side of the open spread, each page will be numbered consecutively and the print (in the Western world) will read from left to right. Most people learn this structure from the age of three onwards, and it would never occur to them to question it. An exhibition has none of these conventions, so visitors must be given a visually strong, subconsciously recognizable framework to enable them to find a pattern. Then they can follow the information effectively through the display area.

Information and words go hand in hand. It is almost, though not quite, impossible to communicate without them. There is a danger at this stage for those involved with commercial exhibitions to lose interest in this chapter. Please do not. No exhibition can get by without words and, instead of treating them casually, it is worth reflecting that even one or two words are better well presented than badly presented.

The print

The letters that make the words have to be manufactured and generally printed. We read words by noticing several different elements. We read the letters, we read the shape of the whole word, we read the size of the word and we read it in direct relationship to its fellows. A letter is read by its shape. The outlines of e, a, o and q can be confused; so can r and n. Words made entirely of capitals (UPPER CASE) have a less easily recognized shape than those made of upper and lower case. The former, with no tall letters (risers or ascenders) or tails below the line (descenders) are not as easily read as the latter. On this page, over which you have total control, the difference is not vital but in an exhibition where the visitor might be tired, jostled by the crowd and at the wrong distance, it becomes very important. If a fascia or title board on an exhibition is limited in size, it would therefore be well to use upper and lower case rather than the apparently more obvious capitals, in order that they should be legible from a greater distance. However, if the capitals are accompanied by an easily-recognizable **logo**, the problem is solved.

An easily-seen and remembered logo.

Typefaces, too, make a great difference to perception. A serif is a short extra line on the arms of a letter. This **E** has six little extra lines, as opposed to this sans serif **E**. On closely packed pages such as this one, the serif brings order, character and fluidity to the text and helps the eye along. Tests have shown that sans serif is slightly harder to read on a book page. The opposite is true if the eye is a long distance from the words, when serifs can blur the profile of a word and make it more difficult to distinguish.

Weight and spacing

The weight of the print is another factor of importance. Most typefaces come in several standard packages: **condensed**, **light**, **medium**, **bold** and **italic**, but not all typefaces come in all packages. Correct contrast between the background and the weight of the print is important – too much contrast, like driving into bright sunlight, is eventually disturbing; too little is like driving at dusk. With white out of black, or reverse lettering – not the easiest of reading circumstances – a light typeface will disappear. If it is **back-lit**, bold lettering may glare. It is always best to use a heavier type than seems to be needed under reverse circumstances; so for light use medium, and never use condensed type.

The spacing between the letters is crucial. It is a part of the reading process to recognize spaces: 'at' presents a familiar shape; 'a t' is unfamiliar, and confusion will reign between where one word ends and another begins. Spacing between the lines is impor-

UPPER CASE

lower case

E

Serif

E

Sans serif

Condensed

light

medium

bold

italic

reversed out

Close letter spacing, normal leading

Exhibitions come in all shapes and sizes.
Resultantly, they mean many different things
to different people.

Very close letter spacing, normal leading

Exhibitions come in all shapes and sizes.
Resultantly, they mean many different things
to different people.

Normal letter spacing, normal leading

Exhibitions come in all shapes and sizes.
Resultantly, they mean many different things
to different people.

Normal letter spacing, increased leading

Exhibitions come in all shapes and sizes.
Resultantly, they mean many different things
to different people.

tant. It is called 'leading', after the amount of lead the old-fashioned printer would put between one line and the next. Leading should be slightly deeper in an exhibition than on the printed page and line lengths should be shorter: 50 characters maximum. The reason for both these factors is again to do with standing in an exhibition; it is impossible to stand completely still without support. The eye traverses a line, comes to the end and then flicks back and down to the next line. If the lines are too long and too densely packed, the eye quite simply gets lost on the way back and cannot find the correct place. At this point, the exhibition audience is lost. This is not psychology but fact, well remarked and recorded for instance by Herbert Spencer and Linda Reynolds, and information of great value. In the restless environment of an exhibition even a few words, a title, a description of a piece of machinery or a label on a photograph must be as easily received as possible.

Blocks of text

We have dealt with letters, words, lines and spaces. The next item is blocks of text or paragraphs. Long paragraphs are daunting because of the apparent mass of information, and they also make it easier for the traversing eye to get lost. Start with very short paragraphs, clearly separated. Build up, but not too much, to longer paragraphs. Shape is clearly important, too; blocks of text are either justified (forming a straight edge to the left and right, as on this page) or ranged left or right (straight edge to one side only, ragged on the other). Finally, they can be centred (lined up equally on either side). Short line lengths of justified type look awful in the larger sizes used in exhibitions; they do not look too good in newspapers, either! The uneven spacing between words stands out a mile. Ranged left looks good, with the ragged right-hand edge balanced by the neat left-hand edge.

If paragraphs are indented (the first line cut in by a few characters), then both sides can look messy. It is better to allow a one-line space between paragraphs instead. Centring can be useful, particularly when fitting text into circles or ellipses. Ranging right always looks odd, but it can be used to balance an unwieldy **panel**.

Ranged left...

Exhibitions come in all shapes and sizes. Resultantly, they mean many different things to different people. It is not even possible to be too specific about what the word 'exhibition' means, as it is one of those words which have several public meanings and even more 'professional' ones.

Ranged right...

Exhibitions come in all shapes and sizes. Resultantly, they mean many different things to different people. It is not even possible to be too specific about what the word 'exhibition' means, as it is one of those words which have several public meanings and even more 'professional' ones.

Centred

Exhibitions come in all shapes and sizes. Resultantly, they mean many different things to different people. It is not even possible to be too specific about what the word 'exhibition' means, as it is one of those words which have several public meanings and even more 'professional' ones.

Indented paragraph

Surprisingly enough, at the time of writing, this is the one area of exhibition design still dominated by amateurs.
Exhibitions, shows, displays, fairs are all words used to mean the same sort of thing

Line space between paragraphs

Surprisingly enough, at the time of writing, this is the one area of exhibition design still dominated by amateurs.

Exhibitions, shows, displays, fairs are all words used to mean the same sort of thing

There are no strict rules to govern the number of words in a block of main text; it rather depends upon where the text is. This leads us back to the hierarchies mentioned earlier. At a primary level there should be no paragraphs at all: just titles and headings or headlines. A secondary level might present one small and one larger paragraph, say one hundred words in all. At the tertiary level, depending upon how evident the text is, quite a few paragraphs might be used. If the tertiary level is only accessed through a computer and there are plenty of them, there is really no limit.

Scale and distance

The size of the display itself is patently another controlling factor when it comes to the number of words. We have all heard stories about the Lord's Prayer being printed on the head of a pin. They are doubtless true, but then no normally sighted person would be able to read it. It is clearly possible to print as much as one likes on to an exhibit label, but if the label is 400 mm square and beside an object 450 mm behind a piece of glass and the print is 2 mm high, most people will be unable to read it, or will bang their heads on the glass in attempting to do so. This page is controlled by you, the reader. The viewers in the exhibition are controlled by the designer and the people around them. The print must be big enough to be read by the normally sighted, the myopic, long-sighted, or middle-aged and elderly.

The Lord's Prayer on a printing block approximately 4 mm square.

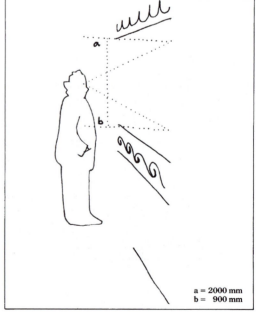

a = 2000 mm
b = 900 mm

a = 2000 mm; b = 900 mm.

Thus the scale/distance factor is vital and can only be truly assessed by experiment, for illegibility of print varies from typeface to typeface. The size will also be affected by the ideal viewing distance of the object. Pick up a pen, a ring, a cup or any nearby object and examine it; now measure its distance from your eye – probably between 300 and 400 mm. This distance varies enormously from object to object. If there is a label describing something, it should manifestly be placed next to it with a reading distance that corresponds to the viewing distance. Some parts of a large object need to be examined closely, so there is a good reason for a large, remote label or title with a small relevant label beside a detailed part.

Rhythm and consistency

All these factors need to be considered. In fact the whole exhibition should be designed with an informative or graphic rhythm which will lead to a regular and easily-understood environment. To this end, a set of standardized typefaces and sizes will be selected for one exhibition in the same way as it is has been for this book. Main titles, headings, headlines, sub-heads and text at levels two and three will all conform to specific sizes selected to accommodate viewing distances. The main title may conform to other main titles, or be contrived to attract attention by being strikingly different.

The presentation of words is therefore not simple. It is complex in order to make the enjoyment of an exhibition simple for the visitor. Failure to interest visitors will send them to other museums, galleries and exhibitions or to McDonald's.

A heavy-handed and dull government information display without any obvious rhythm.

Untidy, overbearing graphics to which, not surprisingly, nobody is paying any attention.

Type production

How are the words produced for an exhibition? At one time they were printed by conventional methods, and then photocopied into sizes and on to materials suitable for exhibitions. Production methods and technology are changing and generally improving continually, so too detailed a discussion of this item is pointless. At the time of writing pasted-up artwork produced by a graphic designer has virtually disappeared. The contractors who reproduce words or graphics for an exhibition use equipment that requires all typesetting, drawings and photographs to be supplied on a disk in digital form. This requires the graphic designer to be not only familiar with graphic layout for an exhibition, but also with the type of computers that produce the necessary electronic format on disk.

Craftsmen working on cut-out brass letters.

Fret-cut lettering where the body of the letter is removed.

In display circumstances there are, however, still needs for fairly conventionally produced graphics. The most primitive method of reproducing words at a large scale for titles or sub-titles is using **cut-out letters**. These are cut from sheets of cork, plywood, metal or plastic and painted before or after mounting them on fascias, walls or panels. It is an effective, if crude, method. The cutting precludes really good **typography**, but offers freedom of siting and layout. Fret-cutting letter shapes from a panel (leaving a hole the shape of the letter) is another good idea, but a clear plastic or glass sheet has to be glued to the back of fret-cut letters, otherwise the centres of the letters o and a will fall out!

These panels are generally back-lit. Cut-out and **fret-cut** letterings do not really involve printing. The remaining techniques do, even signwriting or hand-painting letters on to a surface – always executed by a skilled signwriter. The latter is an expensive, time-consuming business, but sometimes called for.

Signwriting. An ancient and skilled craft still used today.

In large areas of brightly-lit informative displays, colour – for instance brown printed on to beige – is far less aggressive than black on white, and therefore less difficult to read. It can be used both for applying graphic rhythm and for punctuation. For example, headings could be printed in one colour, text in another, and words which might merit quotation marks printed in another colour. Captions to pictures or diagrams might be printed in a different colour, thus separating body text from labels. Using both these methods imaginatively can lead to a well-ordered and attractive display, encouraging the visitor to take an interest in the information presented *and* making it easy to follow.

'Britain Before Man', Geological Museum, 1977. The tonal differences shown here were colour in reality to unify the graphics and help in the rhythmic flow of information.

Order and decoration

Order is of course important, but too much is sterile and forbidding. Again balance is the thing and, if deemed necessary, decoration. When a mass of information is presented, too much order can make it sinister and dull.

When it is chaotic, it looks like hard work. A median path must be sought by the graphic designer in conjunction with the three-dimensional designer. There is a band of normal vision from 900 mm to 2000 mm from the floor which should normally contain all detailed information; decoration can emphasize that band and ensure that the eye stays within it or, when required, rise above or sink below it.

Order should also be sustained when it comes to labels and captions. All captions should be of a similar character and length and always appear in the same relationship to the object throughout any given exhibition. All labels should present their information in the same order and style, and also relate similarly to the objects.

Decoration can emphasize order but must never be used on a whim, for one person's decoration is another's ghastly mess. It is an insupportable argument if taste is the only criterion. Taste, as a word, is meaningless because it conveys something different from every speaker to every listener. It is a word abused by overuse. When decoration is employed it is there for a purpose: to enliven thematically a poorly illustrated story; to delineate chapters of the story; to enable the important graphics to override a dull shell scheme or system; or to create a special, individual atmosphere.

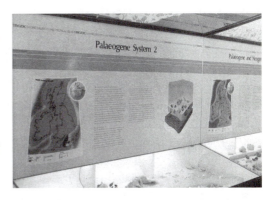

'British Fossils', Geological Museum, 1980. Decoration used to separate tiers in a hierarchy of information.

Decoration should be restrained, and used always slightly less than required. If the decoration dominates the information, the message will be lost. Exhibitions are not for designers to show everybody how clever they are.

Decoration used to emphasize the boundaries of important information.

Tonal differences again were colour in reality to brighten an otherwise dull display.

Detailed presentation

All text, and the objects and pictures associated with it, should be presented at easy
right angles to the eye. This means that if
the visitor has to look down or up to 'read',
the displays should remain at right angles
to the eye.

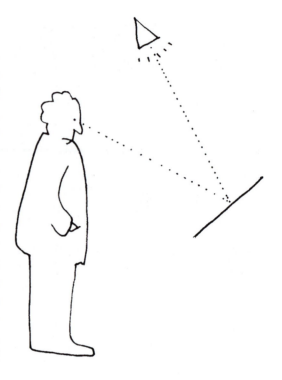

Once any angles are involved, the relationship of light sources to these flat planes
becomes important, in order that reflections or glare can be avoided. Pictures are
associated with text in a number of ways:
they can be mounted on independent
blocks and then placed on a wall; they can
be mounted on panels with the text on a
strip below; or they can have the text over-
printed. With contemporary technology,
they can all be assembled in a variety of
ways on the same panel.

Composition

All pictures have a compositional direction. A well-composed diagram or picture will draw
the eye to the centre, the point of sharpest vision and therefore detail. Many photographs,
however, have an implied direction. The most obvious is when it is of something that
moves: an animal, car or ship, for instance. The eye will be led in the direction of normal
movement. Some compositions have a strong, dark form to one side with perspective lines
leading arrow-like to a pale sky on the other; this 'arrow' is subliminally perceived. Such
markers should be used to lead the visitor's eye smoothly in the direction of the information run (left to right in the West, for we read from left to right).

Clearly there is scope for a whole book about exhibition graphics which goes into
detail about design, typography, reproduction methods and techniques. This chapter
attempts only to be a guide for a three-dimensional exhibition designer to the understanding of a need for professional graphic design input, as well as a knowledge of how
to brief, control and supervise the graphics to create a harmonious whole. Whereas it is
usually the three-dimensional designer who accepts a brief for an exhibition, it is valuable
if a graphic designer is consulted at the earliest possible moment; in fact, as soon as a
three-dimensional form to the exhibition emerges. In this way, the graphic input will be
sympathetic and relevant.

A picture that would look uneasy on the left of a display panel but fine on the right.

A well-composed if uninspiring picture where the eye is led peacefully towards the centre.

Fashion

This is a good point at which to consider one aspect of design that strongly affects both three-dimensional and graphic design: fashion. This plays an important role in the commercial and aesthetic part of our lives. However, it is transient. Its transience and immediate relevance must therefore be clearly considered and either dismissed or used. If an exhibition is to be permanent, then it is far more important that it should 'look' aesthetically relevant for as long as possible. The same applies to the graphics in the exhibition, for there are distinct fashions in typeface and style of embellishment. If a 'timeless' design is attempted for an exhibition, then the graphics will let it down if full of fashionable typefaces and quirks. Typefaces should be selected for their stylistic relevance to the subject and decoration should be designed similarly. It is, of course, almost impossible to exclude fashion from any design but it should, in these permanent circumstances, be only a gentle reminder of the period of execution and not a dominant statement.

When a temporary structure is envisaged, fashion can be used and even graphics and decoration set in the style. When a very recent development is being exhibited, it is positively beneficial for the exhibition to be as stylish as possible, thus reflecting the modernity of the product and the company image. These are two clear examples; the sensitive

A stand designed deliberately to reflect the fashion of the late 1960s and thus give decimalization a thoroughly modern image.

and imaginative designer will be aware of fashion and use it – or, with luck, create it – to serve the purpose of the exhibition.

Words are fundamental ingredients of exhibition design. This chapter has attempted to explain that both the content and the presentation of words should be considered by the designer from the earliest point of involvement. It is useless to discuss them as an unfortunate necessity, to be added as crude labels or stuck on displays at the last moment. They should be integrated and homogeneous. The plan, the very layout of the exhibition, should harmonize with the informative content to this end.

An entire chapter has been devoted to the detailed discussion of words in an exhibition, and their importance cannot be over-stated. A number of exhibition designers consider words to be almost irrelevant, while an equal number of exhibitors believe words to be the most important part of a display. In 1985 the Boilerhouse, a specialist design gallery in the Victoria and Albert Museum at the time, had an introductory panel containing 2000 words – the equivalent of a sizeable magazine article. It was presumably considered essential reading for the poor visitor on entering the exhibition. Both extremes are of course absurd. A happy balance has to be achieved; objects relative to each other can 'speak' volumes. A sequence of real examples of all stages in the production of a ceramic jug, for instance, will make a fascinating explanatory display with practically no words at all.

A clearly absurd exhibition design, wherein only a few of the showcases come anywhere near acceptable viewing or label-reading heights. 'Hand Tools' exhibition at the Boilerhouse, 1984.

Similar relative displays can be made under countless circumstances, and any display which allows or encourages the visitor to explore and discover visually rather than literally is exactly suitable for exhibition purposes. Long explanations beg the need for an exhibition at all; perhaps a book would have been better.

6 The principles

AT this stage the practical basis for design should be examined. Designing is problem solving. No problem can be effectively dealt with until it has been defined. Chapter 4 attempted to set out the essential elements of the problem, and the design process logically follows from that. There is, and always will be, one imponderable element among those under consideration: the visitor, the person for whom the exhibition is ultimately designed. Research is going on to attempt to describe the potential behaviour of this elusive creature and this will be discussed in a later chapter, but it is vital for the designer to remember that the most valuable tool available when it comes to visitor assessment is personal observation. Observation, used constructively, is essential to good design. It is one thing to skim through glossy magazines on a search for ideas or stimulation, but it is quite another to visit exhibitions and notice both the design and the visitors' reactions to it. Habitual observation of this kind will build up a valuable body of experience, often described as intuition but actually priceless knowledge – which cannot be categorized as scientific knowledge.

The danger with scientifically-acquired information based on visitor questioning is that it is inevitably subjective (two people cannot communicate without a whole substratum of influences) and assumed to be fact. The danger with observed information is that it is assumed to be guesswork. There is an area of visitor research waiting to be undertaken where careful observations by designers are scientifically recorded and prepared. Meanwhile, however, the total use of three-dimensional space must be planned effectively.

Planning

For the sake of this chapter, planning means two slightly separate things: the first is the consideration that goes into the preparation of the layout of an exhibition; the second is the straightforward business of preparing scale drawings and fitting on to them the necessary solids and spaces to form an exhibition.

Public space

This is the area of the exhibition devoted to the movement and use of the public. It must be easily and immediately accessible, and it must be big enough for them. Most doorways, for example, are big enough for people to pass through alone but not really for people to

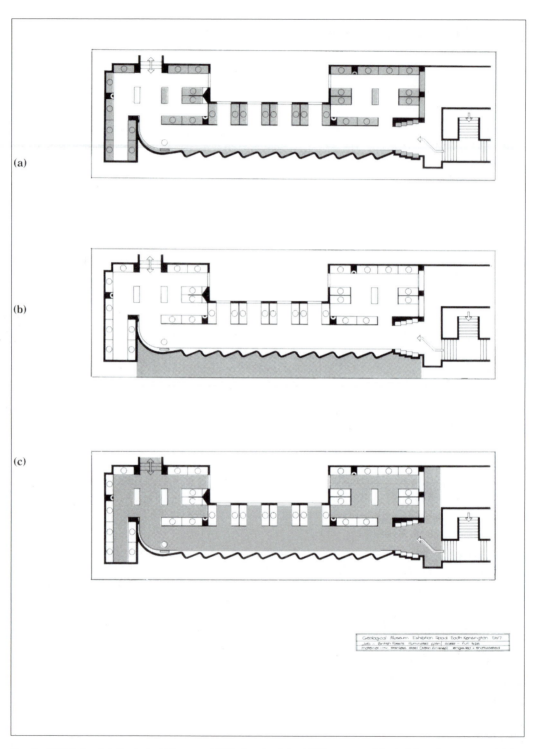

Plan for 'British Fossils', Geological Museum, 1980, showing (a) exhibition space, (b) administrative space and (c) public space.

pass each other. There are books about 'human dimensions', but sheer common sense and a measuring tape dictate the width of an aisle in which one person may be standing, looking or bending to look, while two others are passing behind; a visitor in a wheelchair will need even more space. There must also be room for people to talk and to exchange information without disturbing the solitary viewer.

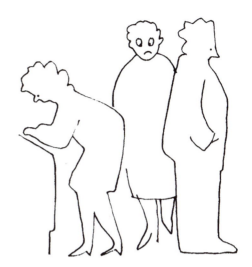

Informative space

This is the actual exhibition space for objects, models, **artefacts**, showcases, **light-boxes** and vertical or sloping flat displays. Obviously the available space is somewhat controlled by the size of the objects on display. Moreover it must be planned with its informative and attractive values in mind; if all the most inviting objects are placed on the edge of an exhibition, the visitor is going to be very disappointed when moving into the duller spaces beyond. Size is important, of course; huge objects can obscure small ones. Safety is important; if working exhibits are involved there must be a barrier and a space between them and the visitor.

Administrative space

This is space set aside for many vital purposes out of direct reach or sight of the public. It is space for access for maintenance, changing bulbs behind transparencies or lamps for projectors, or attending to working exhibits or models. Many exhibitions have **counters** where administrative space meets **public space**; these must be adroitly sited and ought to be provided with solid fronts, so that tired attendants can relax their legs and feet out of sight of the visitor. Administrative space can be divided as detailed below.

Space for storage
Many temporary exhibitions are backed up with **literature** and samples to be given away, so an assessment of these needs is important.

Space for staff
Most temporary exhibitions have attendant managers and representatives who need room to relax, loosen smart clothing for a while, have a cup of tea or change into uniforms. No

matter how small the stand, such space is vital. On huge temporary stands – at world fairs, for example – this space can run into a sizeable proportion of the whole area, calling for toilets and washrooms, offices, changing rooms and kitchens.

Entertainment space
Additional space might be required for important customers to be given special treatment, such as drinks or private video shows.

Types of plan

Essentially, there are two broad types of arrangement: **extrovert** and **introvert**.

The extrovert exhibition
This type is built on an island or near-island all to itself, either in an exhibition hall, a museum or an outdoor site. At their grandest, these extrovert exhibitions could be pavil-ions at world fairs. This is a form of design which appeals for attention from all sides and is frequently open to the public on all sides. Its displays are designed to attract the public 'on board', as it were. In exhibition halls these stands can be double-deckers, two- or even three-floored structures presenting vast and exotic façades to compete with their neigh-

The exterior of the Millennium Dome during construction in 1999. The buses indicate the scale.

bours in attracting public attention. If they present huge blank walls to the public, they are denying the value of the island site (which costs more to rent); therefore the space should be either at the heart or upper level of such a stand, or on an unimportant elevation. Every aspect of the design should encourage the public to visit. This type of design can be difficult to supervise, not only from the point of view of security, but also from the commercial standpoint. It is essential that every visitor be visible to the stand staff, who can then approach at the right moment if a sale looks possible. Stands of this nature are frequently costly affairs, so the financial burden of extra staff with their attendant travel and subsistence requirements ought to be considered at the outset.

The introvert exhibition

This type presents less of a problem for supervision. It refers to an exhibition designed into an existing space – a booth at a trade fair; a room or suite of rooms in a museum, gallery or hotel. Here there are only internal spaces and surfaces to be thought about, with possibly only one outside elevation. As the visitors come and go, they pass either through the front of the booth or the entrance and exit to the rooms. In an introvert exhibition, the challenge is to get the visitors through the entrance and, once there, to keep them inter-

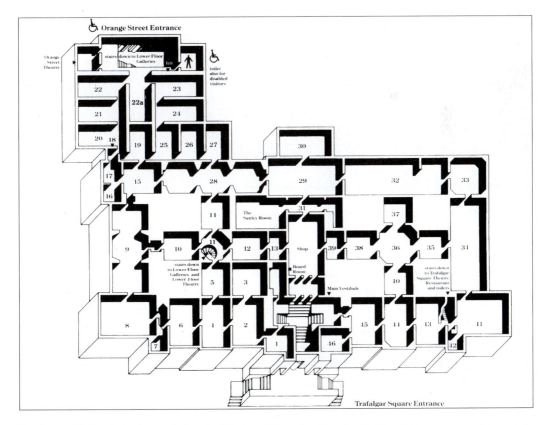

The National Gallery in London excluding the Sainsbury Wing. A gallery plan that inevitably encourages introverted exhibitions.

Entrance to the Play Zone in the Millennium Dome, 2000, by Land Design Studio.

ested since it is not so easy to leave the area. This is particularly true in a suite of adjoining rooms in a gallery. Some galleries, the Royal Academy in London, for instance, were deliberately designed with interconnecting spaces, often on four sides. This facilitates the design of temporary exhibitions, all introverted, of many sizes; rooms are sealed off or included as and when required.

The author was able, due to small and late involvement with one of the areas, to see the Millennium Dome in its last few months of construction, and to visit it on one of the preview days. It is interesting to note that most of the advice contained in the above and following paragraphs was certainly not heeded, and more likely not even read. Time will tell if the Dome was a success, but to build any structure before defining clearly its purpose would seem to the author to be ill-advised. Furthermore, because it was a tent two of the main advantages of enclosed space were lost: first, there was far too much light during daylight hours to exploit exciting lighting effects; and second, it was impossible to hang any exciting structures using invisible wires (sky-hooks) from overhead.

As far as the content was concerned, when the various areas were being conceived they all turned out to be attempting to express ideas, ideology and concepts, and with the exception of one or two zones most attempts to turn such things into attractive exhibits did not work. The exteriors of a number of structures or zones were designed by architects who were not used to the lack of the exciting play on good architecture of **chiaroscuro**. Thus in the monotone circumstances of the Dome such structures looked very bland. Nor did they seem to be aware of the need for their structures to be positively inviting. Only those designed by exhibition designers exploited techniques that made the exteriors attractive. In the simple slang of the exhibition profession, most of the Dome was a 'book-on-legs'.

Planning considerations

These comprise a necessary part of the definition of the problem, for they will inevitably effect the plan and shape of the exhibition.

Supervision

The importance of supervision has already been mentioned. In the late 1960s it meant simply that it had to be possible to see all parts of an exhibition from one or two vantage points, so that in the commercial venue visitors could be persuaded to buy by the sales-men. In recent years supervision has come to mean guarding against vandals and, at worst, terrorists. A well-designed exhibition is one whose sales and/or security staff can see through, round or over the exhibits and the informative space. In museums and galleries this function is now assisted by the use of closed circuit television (CCTV), but whilst cameras may act as a deterrent to some it should be remembered that no matter how many cameras are used, CCTV is only as efficient as the members of staff viewing the screen.

Control

One other effect arises from this consideration. Convoluted plans are tiresome for the visitor. He or she is not there to try and find the way around, but to be easily confronted by the things the exhibitor wants to be seen and appreciated. If it is made difficult, the visitor will not bother – therefore there are good and bad plans. Good and bad are, of course, emotive and subjective words, but such plans exist and have nothing to do with taste. A good plan is either subconsciously or consciously easy to follow; visitors know where they are, relative to the exhibition and the world outside, feel consequently more at ease, and so more receptive to the information displayed. It should always be possible for visitors to identify familiar landmarks. They then remain oriented and in control. Exhibits should be placed in a logical sequence. All subjects have information patterns or structures to their description, and once the designer and client have arrived at one such pattern it should be adhered to. A petrol engine, for instance, can be described historically by its evolution from invention to the present day; or sociologically through the immense variety of its uses and its effect on society; or chemically by referring to the component minerals that go to make it up. Clearly, one or more of these information patterns will be relevant to its presence on display and pertinent to the story being told. Accordingly the objects on display relevant to the engine must be laid out in the proper order.

Confusion eventually leads to despair, and a despairing visitor makes a very poor customer. This confusion is rampant in a bad plan. Such a plan will be disconcerting and maze-like. It could be dauntingly large with no clear sign of display activity, so that it is difficult for the visitor to know whether or not entry is allowed, whether or not to touch. A bad plan shows no clear difference between public, exhibit and administrative space and it is full of apparent blind alleys or cul-de-sacs. The administrative space can be so forbidding and vast that it presents a grim exterior to the public, even if sounds of hilarity can be heard from behind the wall. A bad plan ought to be evident on the drawing board or screen. A good plan will elevate well from the drawing to the site, to present a friendly and receptive structure in which the assimilation of information comes naturally and easily to the visitor.

Vertical treatment

Limitless height is not a commodity generally available to the exhibition designer, and even if it were it would not be of any great value except as a place in which to indicate one's presence. The vital thing to remember with **vertical space** is that the more there is of it, the further away the visitor has to be in order to see it. The Eiffel Tower, that ultimate exhibition feature, can be seen in grossly distorted detail from close to, and only in the most general possible way from a distance of about a mile. There is no in-between. If you wanted to study its complex structure about halfway

The first of Man's aspiring exhibition features, but you have to be a long way off to see it properly.

up, you would have to contrive all sorts of devices to enable you to do so.

Average **eye level** is considered to be about 1600 mm above floor level. If a vertical display panel is approximately a metre high and a metre off the ground, the viewer will have to be about a metre away from it to view or 'read' a square metre of it comfortably. If the display has to start near floor level and rise to three metres up, then it must first be seen from at least three metres away. After the initial vertical appreciation, the visitor can move in closely to examine it in more detail.

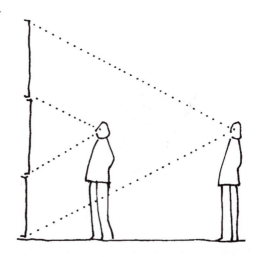

If there is no way that the correct viewing distance can be provided, then there is no point in putting on such a display, except in those instances where the sheer scale of an object can be emphasized by exaggeration when it is placed in close confines. Obviously in the exhibition context, vertical and horizontal space is inextricably intertwined and, as was seen in the previous chapter, readability of words has a considerable effect on the acceptability or otherwise of certain contrived spaces.

Horizontal treatment

Horizontal space is not divided up necessarily by solid verticals, solid walls or solid exhibits; transparent or semi-open walls and objects are generally far friendlier things than the opaque materials that are usually found in buildings. **Double-sided** showcases can also form divisions, as can low horizontal cases or displays; thus a plan, a devised flow of visitors in certain informative directions, can generally be contrived as much by the placement of objects as by the placement of artificial walls and open or solid **partitions**.

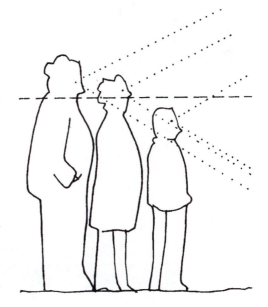

It is this use of vertical space that, mixed with a well-devised plan, allows for two of the most important elements in any exhibition: fluid circulation and ease of

Average eye level is said to be about 1600 mm from the floor. It does not suit everybody, but nothing is perfect.

supervision. Fluid circulation is vital for the comfortable and logical reception of information in space. Good supervision is vital to the exhibition staff to avoid missing customers, and to security staff so that if the occasion arises they can prevent damage or theft. Of course, if the potential thief or vandal never feels alone, he is unlikely to attempt anything.

Cleverly contrived double-sided showcases. 'Man's Place in Evolution', British Museum (Natural History), 1980.

The exhibits

Without objects, there would be no need for this book. Exhibitions are essentially about objects. In the museum context they are paramount, for it is only in museums that the image-saturated and more or less sedentary public can see, relate to and sometimes touch things they have read about or seen pictures of elsewhere. A museum exhibition without objects is therefore almost offensive and its *raison d'être* must be questioned. Where what is clearly only a words-and-pictures narrative to be told in a three-dimensional situation, models and **replicas** have to be made in the absence of artefacts.

In the commercial or prestige exhibition, objects lend integrity and interest to the statements made about them, but paradoxically it is frequently the statements which are most important. The visitor is therefore drawn to the statements through the objects. A car is a car is a car, but the facts about fuel consumption, power and performance can only be stated and not tested by the visitor. It is the gleaming, polished example that attracts atten-

Standing the world on its side to emphasize a point.

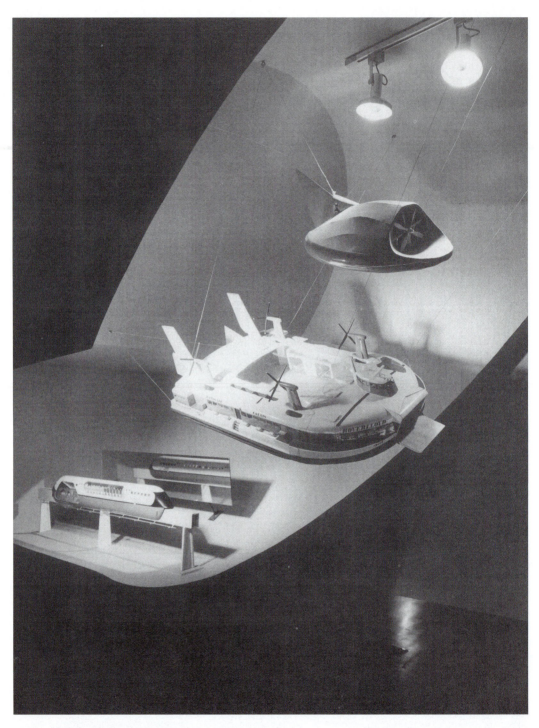

Scale models lending drama to a display.

Paraded in the showroom, the car will attract attention . . .

tion to these important selling points. At a prestige exhibition, a national pavilion, for example, products of the nation – even if only beautifully displayed – give the attendant statements an air of conviction. A pavilion totally devoid of objects of this kind occasionally can be of interest, but it is rare. The average visitor does not pay the entrance fee, and travel sometimes hundreds of miles, only to be told something which could easily be read in a magazine, encyclopaedia or on the Internet.

There is a magical quality to displayed objects, which is hard to explain. An ordinary car, polished, tilted and lit for display has a charisma quite unlike that of the very same vehicle parked in the road.

The size or **scale** of exhibits is also important. The very large and the very small always create a peculiar interest. Their **context** is equally important. A very large object on a huge exhibition stand will simply look normal, but if it is apparently cramped in, its scale will be exaggerated. Similarly, very small objects shown individually in special cases will have their smallness and their value enhanced by this special treatment. **Massing** ordinary objects also gives them a special charm.

Chinese national pavilions over the years have ignored contemporary display techniques and shown the variety and interest of their products by massing them on tiered displays like Victorian grocers' shops. The sheer quantity and neatness of the goods seem to add to their quality, while emphasizing the productivity of the country of origin. Contrast emphasizes size. Magnified models of small objects or small models of huge things always

. . . while in the street it is not given a second glance.

generate interest and, as all movement attracts the eye, making all objects of all sizes revolve is another way of emphasizing their qualities and attracting attention. We have all experienced the great delight of examining exquisitely detailed workmanship, and it is building valuable information upon these pleasurable responses that makes for good exhibition display.

Information

Information must be the basis upon which all exhibition planning eventually takes place. After all the practical considerations, it is the information that decides the general layout. The synopsis of the information provided with the brief must be clear and sufficiently finalized for the layout to be decided at a comparatively early stage.

Which is more attractive, the display or the objects on display?

There are two fundamental ways of displaying or retailing information (other, of course, than chaotically or informally): a **systematic** display will be laid out in some explicit order – chronological, scientific, biological or evolutionary; a **thematic** display will be laid out as a story, around a central theme. There has been a strong move towards essentially thematic displays in recent years. 'Story' titles make evocative and inviting exhibition themes. Moreover they provide something for the visitor's imagination to dwell upon. The two methods can easily be mixed so that a thematic exhibition, built around a theme or story, can be chronologically ordered. This ordering of the exhibition will obviously affect the planning of the exhibition site. Even the very smallest booth will need to have the layout of the information considered, but clearly the larger and more complex the site, the more important the logical layout becomes. On an island site, a logical plan can be difficult to achieve since the visitors will approach from all directions, so various devices have to be contrived to encourage passage in the direction the designer wants. The best way of achieving this is to place the most eye-catching display at the beginning of the story. It must be attractive – literally in the way that a lighted candle attracts a moth. Having attracted the visitor in this way, the problem is only partly solved; he or she must then be encouraged to proceed in the direction of the informative path by orienting displays in such a manner that can be followed easily. With a systematic display on an island site, the information can be placed in concentric circles around the exhibition in such a way that the starting or ending place does not really matter.

A visitor cannot easily be coerced; the public responds badly to formalized and compulsory routes. People bunch up in the least expected places, and the end result, in a popular exhibition, is a strictly controlled queue: not the best way to sell products or to

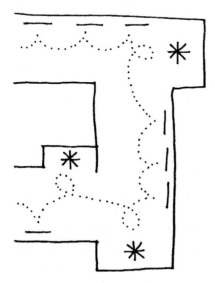

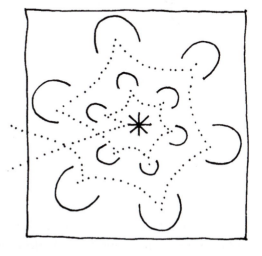

The visitor will be attracted by powerful displays (*) and pictures or text panels leading from left to right.

The visitor will be attracted by a powerful central display (*) and will then move outwards past other highlights, not too apparent from the outside.

encourage learning. At world fairs, this bunched queuing has become almost a way of life in the more popular pavilions, though the public at world fairs is often of the least discrim-inating kind. It is nevertheless bad design to create a situation in which people – no matter how sheepishly – plod slowly around any exhibition, being forced to see the displays at the pace of the queue and not at their own. Freedom of movement through objects and infor-mation should be fundamental to good design. It is not only bad design to end up with such a queue, but also bad co-ordination between the publicists and the organizers. Frequently an exhibition is 'hyped' way beyond its ability to cope (the Body Zone at the Millennium Dome). The organizers and sponsors delightedly see huge queues forming to see their exhibition, but it is questionable whether such a solid phalanx of eventually cross and uncomfortable visitors is actually good publicity at all. To be forced to stand in front of the same scene that one may not particularly like cannot, in the long term, leave one with a kindly feeling.

Illustration

Illustrations form a fundamental part of any exhibition. To many people, exhibitions are simply about pictures, but it is the picture which is on exhibition in its own right. Pictures also play what might be termed secondary and tertiary roles. The secondary role is when pictures of the exhibits are on display. One fine object is backed up by photographs of other varieties or types of the same thing. The tertiary role is when they form part of the background to, or explanation of, the objects. Pictures in the primary role, as in an art exhibition, are generally seen to be outside the remit of the designer. In this context, the design brief may be simply to create a tasteful, well-lit background while others – art histo-rians, for example – take care of the hanging within the shell that the designer has created. This can lead to a situation where the exhibition is totally out of control. Pictures are placed within their historical context perhaps, but their placement bears no relation to the actual planning of the exhibition. If the designer does not know the whereabouts of this or that picture, with this or that viewing distance and pulling power, it is impossible to plan an exhibition to function satisfactorily.

Any exhibition is a machine for enlightenment. If the working parts are simply thrown together on the ground, how can it possibly work? With a few notable exceptions, exhibi-tions of fine art in the UK have virtually all been chaotic, inhospitable environments wherein the public struggles for information, in circumstances arranged to please an élite few who only experience the exhibition in the comfort of a private view.

Pictures in their secondary or tertiary roles are in the place where we start to get involved with the nitty-gritty of **informative display**. Everything so far in this chapter has been in general terms, but when discussing the process of actually informing the visitor with pictures and objects, we need to talk about the actual methods of presenting them.

Photographs

The simplest and cheapest method is the photograph, black and white, mounted on board at a standard size.

It is clearly worth spending a bit of money, first of all, on using colour, and secondly on enlarging the photograph at least to a suitable viewing size relative to the object it adjoins. Of course, enlargements can be taken to glorious extremes, depending on paper size, but it must be remembered that the quality of the original **negative** becomes more and more critical the bigger the enlargement becomes. A 35 mm negative, enlarged to 2 m wide, becomes very grainy, which is acceptable provided that effect only is required and the visitor is not expected to examine it closely for detailed information. These enlargements are generally on plastic-coated paper, mounted on to panels. The paper comes only in specified widths, so the joints in the enlargement over a certain size have

A photograph enlarged for background effect.

to be considered. The length of the rolls of paper is generally unlimited, so only one set of joints has to be watched. If they are lit along the seam, there will be no shadow, but if light falls across the seam the joint can become quite obvious. It is also possible to enlarge on to transparent plastic film, either for normal viewing or for back lighting. The size of these plastic sheets again varies, but they are usually a great deal larger and costlier than photographic paper and require a strong supporting frame to stretch the film.

Back-lit **transparencies** on proper film, sandwiched between **opal** and clear glass or **Perspex** sheets and lit with a carefully mounted battery of fluorescent tubes at least 200 mm back from the film, are generally considered to be the best way of showing good quality colour photographs in an exhibition. The size is limited to the sheet film size, so it is generally within the enlargement range of the original negative. However, the bigger the better. Photographs can also be enlarged by computer reading methods on to cloth, stretched or used as a curtain, and carpet. Again, there is a considerable loss of definition, so enlargements of this type can only be used for scene setting or background purposes. Photographs on to cloth have the advantage of being completely non-reflective; there are no high spots of light to irritate the visitor. Other materials that will receive photographs are **plastic laminates**, in which the photograph is printed on to a special tissue and then laminated either into a **thermoplastic** or glass-reinforced plastic. These laminates can be made almost indestructible.

Photographs reproduced in many of

The tri-sign moving picture.

The triangular section horizontal bars (Toblerones©) move through 120 degrees to show three separate pictures in the same space.

the above methods can be moved or interchanged, so that more than one picture can occupy the same apparent space. Prints can be displayed on mechanical **flip-over** panels, virtually a picture book with hard pages, or transparencies can be contained on a long opal reel that, to predetermined pulses, advances picture by picture. One of these devices is a patented French system called **Rotosign**. Pictures can also be mounted on what are called '**toblerones**', after the triangular-sectioned chocolate bars. Either a single picture is mounted on to each face of the toblerone, which revolves mechanically, stopping and starting for each face, or many toblerones can be racked vertically or horizontally with the photograph sliced and mounted on to them. If the whole rack is revolved continuously, the

A photo mural at a commercial exhibition. The Porsche stand at the Motor Show, 1986.

An underwater scene painted on eight layers of acrylic sheet. A glass painting in 'Britain Before Man', Geological Museum, 1977.

changing picture effect can be quite dramatic. This method is also used in a commercial product called **Rotagraphics**, but the 20 mm slats with 2 mm joints degrade the photograph somewhat, so again the viewing distance is important.

Special artwork

While so far only considering photographs, this chapter does of course include pictures, diagrams, maps and so on, often turned into digital images for ease of reproduction. However, such images are not always the solution to the problems of either detailed or background illustration. Murals are often considered to fulfil the need for large scale, scene-setting **artwork** both for commercial ventures and prestige or museum exhibitions.

In scientific or archaeological displays, representation of the scenery or way of life, or artefacts of centuries ago, can often best be expressed in this way. Special artwork is often commissioned from specialist illustrators and mural artists who work closely with academics and reference materials, to produce detailed and accurate representations. **Glass painting**, these days generally hand painted on to clear **acrylic** sheets, gives a three-dimensional effect, sometimes very subtle and full of depth.

They, more than other illustrations, have to be specially lit and the artists themselves often undertake this task. Another form of **flat** illustration frequently used is the **cut-away diagram**, again the work of a specialist. This shows the inner workings of anything from a flea to a diesel engine.

Maps

Maps are often a necessity, either to show distribution networks or natural locations. The normal map, produced by cartographic organizations, is generally quite useless for exhibition purposes, being designed with a totally different reading circumstance in mind; special maps have therefore to be drawn and reproduced using print and details readable at the distances, and scales which obtain the correct effect in the exhibition for which they are planned. Whereas most commercial maps contain a wealth of detail, the exhibition requires only a small proportion of the information available. To obscure the relevant

A map especially simplified for exhibition use.

The detail in a commercial map is generally far too fine for use on a panel in an exhibition.

information with these details is unnecessary and bad practice. It must always be remembered that exhibitions are peculiar places in which to receive information – not at all normal. 'Normal' is television, radio or newspapers and, whereas perhaps half the population of the Western world reads a newspaper daily, and nearly all see television of one sort or another, it is unlikely that half that number of people sees any exhibition in an entire year. The percentages speak for themselves.

Computer display

Meanwhile, through the **television monitor**, computers are playing an ever greater part in the day-to-day lives of the population and these must now be considered to be normal tools of the battery of devices available for communicating in exhibitions. While they can contain words and pictures in one form or another, they can also both control working exhibits and interact with the visitor automatically or by using either a simplified or normal **keyboard**. A **simplified keyboard** can range from a yes/no button to a set of letters and numbers which give access to the information within the computer, or separate picture source, slides, video tape or disk. The Play Zone in the Millennium Dome was exceptional in providing a large number of exciting interactive, digitally-driven exhibits which reacted in real time to the input of visitor.

The eventual result of such developments is that more complex concepts can be explained than has been previously possible. The technology involved is changing almost

An immediately understandable simplified keyboard giving access to a computer.

LAND – Play Zone at the Millennium Dome, 2000.

daily, so any explicit suggestions will undoubtedly go out of date before this book is published.

The designer embarking on the use of computers and video-interactive displays should remember, though, that if there is only one available and it seems to be fun, a crowd of unhappy people will rapidly form a queue impatiently awaiting their turn. Therefore such equipment should only be used when a limited number of specialist visitors are expected, or if there is money and space to provide a larger number of terminals.

Another important factor is the production of suitable **program** material. This should only be done by experts and, again, the exhibition context should be remembered. Information should be given in short doses of a maximum of two minutes' duration. Long descriptions needing continuous perusal are out of the question.

The Internet

In the past few years the Internet has become a part of life for many millions of people and clearly will expand more and more with time. The National Portrait Gallery in London has recently opened an Internet Research facility, but this again is an area where changes are taking place so rapidly that examples of it will be out of date before this book is published. The observant student of exhibitions will need to keep as up to date as possible by visiting new exhibitions as well as reading relevant reviews and critiques. If computer programs are developed for an exhibition, museum or heritage centre gallery, then it is worth considering placing it on the Internet or allowing the Internet to be used as access to further information in a part of the display. Nothing will ever replace the value of seeing, handling and understanding the real thing, the object in front of you, but such access could enhance the display and indeed bring more visitors to the exhibition.

Spoken commentary

Words can be produced in many different ways and, while Chapter 5 dealt with the actual writing of words followed by their production, there is another way – sound in the form of spoken commentary. This divides into three types: general sound where the whole exhibition is addressed, specific sound where only parts of the exhibition contain sound, and individual sound using either **handsets**, **radios** or cassette players carried around an exhibition to receive specific information in specific places. Again, the technology for the devices is advancing daily: radio signals or pulses from **buried loops**, short-wave radio and so on. They are best in the hands of specialist firms that deal with both the production of the programs and the installation. It is important to remember that with both general and specific sound, noise 'leaks' from the environment for which it was created. Many public and commercial exhibition organizers forbid the use of such equipment, particularly near aisles, as it interferes with neighbouring exhibitors. In an enclosed exhibition, sound can become an irritant, so it is again important to use professionals in both its production and projection.

The difference between a commentary spoken and produced by amateurs and that done by a professional actor and producer is enormous. The awful, distressed cadences of 'our managing director', when repeated every few minutes, will lose more customers than they will gain. Professionalism, in all subsidiary disciplines in an exhibition, is worth paying for in the long run.

First and third person interpretation

In the past 10 to 15 years interpretation by professional or amateur actors has moved increasingly into heritage centres and industrial site exhibitions. First person interpretation is when a professional actor adopts the dress and role of an historical character, and remains strictly in character when talking to the visitor. Third person, more often used by amateur actors or volunteers, means that while they wear the correct period clothing, they will talk about the subject or site in the third person. Needless to say, the same criteria of information and script apply to this technique as they do to any other use of words in exhibitions.

7 The techniques

HAVING dealt with the more human aspects of exhibition design it is necessary to look at the techniques, devices or gimmicks that are available to the designer. Inevitably these are being invented as this book progresses. Techniques are the tools of the exhibition designer. Without a full, regularly updated set of tools the **craftsperson** is not going to work at his or her best; similarly the designer who does not regularly familiarize himself by visiting the work of others and looking at all communication technology, with an eye to how it might be able to help in this complex discipline, is not going to be at his or her best. On the other hand, techniques must not rule a project. Design first, then evaluate the techniques that will best express the message. Never fall in love with a new technique and determine to use it for its own sake. Obviously this chapter will be out of date as soon as the book is published; nevertheless, there are a considerable number of well-tried techniques that can be listed here, some surprisingly simple, effective and inexpensive.

Special effects

As more and more mention is made of the specialist, we naturally move on to the area of special effects. The whole business of communicating effectively in an exhibition is beset with problems, the greatest of which is keeping the interest of the visitor in probably the most complex circumstances for communicating yet devised. The difficulty is in exploiting continuously the three dimensions in which the communication takes place. As has often been stated in these pages, the only reason for the exhibition is that 'space' is needed and, once involved in space, it is pointless to fill it up simply with words to form what in the trade are ridiculed as '**books-on-legs**'. It is far easier to read sitting at home or in the office, and if literature is needed to accompany an exhibition, this is where it will eventually either be read or passed over.

All special effects are expensive, however, so careful consideration must be given to the suitability of the effect in the circumstances of the information. To deal with space in the most effective way, various techniques have evolved and will of course go on evolving.

Diorama

One of the earliest display techniques to emerge was the **diorama**. This is a modelled painting. Fake perspectives are cleverly exploited in shallow depth to give the impression of great depth. The whole effect is carefully modelled and realistically painted and set up, occasionally using real objects in the foreground. When well lit and carefully sited, they give an

A 'book-on-legs': the designer's name for an exhibition vastly overstocked with text.

impression of reality frozen in time. These models can vary from life size down to really very small with perhaps a viewing aperture of only half a square metre. But the effect of depth and therefore reality greatly enhances what would otherwise be a dull and formal painting.

A working diorama in particular can have its place in an exhibition. This is a diorama in which the more realistically modelled foreground is made to work or operate in some way, while the accurately perspective background remains static. It can also be a drama in which lights or sequenced lighting effects are used to tell a story. The 'Great Fire of London' in the Museum of London is a famous example where a commentary, sound and light effects create a miniature theatre. For a few minutes it is possible to get some sense of reality of the Great Fire and 'what it was like at the time'.

The viewing angles and viewing distances are important when considering dioramas of any kind; the specialist commissioned to make one should see the actual venue, or at least accurate, detailed drawings of it before commencing work. It should also be decided whether the diorama is to be oriented towards adults or children, or both, as with narrow viewing angles and a small diorama it can be difficult to get people in the right place for the best possible view. Some, particularly landscapes, are best seen at first from a distance, whereas working dioramas with complex effects probably demand a close view. Remember that adults can always bend, but children cannot suddenly grow 450 mm unless steps are provided. Even then, if steps of the wrong height are provided,

An enthralling diorama: the 'Great Fire of London' at the Museum of London.

children will simply block the view of the adults.

Pepper's Ghost

Another old technique is the **Pepper's Ghost**, named after John H. Pepper (1821–1900) who perfected H. Dircks's invention for melodramas on the Victorian stage. A Pepper's Ghost exploits the quality of glass at its most transparent when there is a bright light beyond it, and at its most reflective when there is darkness beyond it. Thus, by adjusting lights and the angle of the glass, it is possible to create the effect of one three-dimensional image replacing another before the eyes of the visitor. By careful interplay of lights, angles, real and

'Treasures of the Earth', Geological Museum, 1985. This display has a very specific viewing position. Simple steps make it possible for everybody to see it.

'Treasures of the Earth', Geological Museum, 1985. On pressing the button the workings of this mine are slowly superimposed over the body of ore underground.

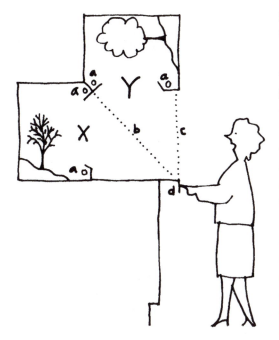

A Pepper's Ghost: a = lights; b = semi-silvered mirror; c=clear glass; d = button which, when pressed, turns lights off in X and lights on in Y. If pressed again it reverses the process. The tree can be seen with or without leaves. The lights can also be faded up and down.

reflected images, it is possible also to create the effect of a '**ghost**' where one image is 'floated' over another. The effect is contrived by the use of **semi-silvered glass**; in other words, glass which is half obscured by fine silvering.

For the technically minded, the effect is achieved by a bright light shining on the real image beyond the glass to give a sharp image, while another bright light is **faded up** or down on to the reflected image. The semi-silvering makes the reflected image quite as sharp as the real image, particularly with the silvered side of the glass closest to the viewer. When the balance of light is totally reversed, so that all light is on the reflected image, the real image completely disappears. Even more so than with dioramas, the **viewing angles** are important – in this case critical – and the exact matching of the two images is a job requiring great skill and meticulous modelling. Pepper's Ghosts can be used, therefore, for showing 'before and after' situations, or for showing two distinct aspects of a complex structure such as the ore body in a mine with a superimposition of the mining shafts and tunnels. Another use, for example, is where an object on display is 'ghosted' in and out of view to be replaced by pictures and text related to it.

There are countless uses for these special effects and, once the imaginative designer has got hold of a new technique, it will undoubtedly be developed further. One such development arose from the need to show a possible career path to teenage visitors. A simple mirror confronted the visitor with the suggestion that he should press a specific button to plan the path of his career; immediately the button was pressed, a pattern of lines emerged over his reflection in the mirror, showing a likely career pattern. This was done simply by using a semi-silvered mirror as the front glass in a transparency, and shining a strong light on the visitor. When the button was pressed, the strong light was dimmed and the transparency illuminated from behind. Again, viewing angles and positions have to be examined. Models, dioramas and Pepper's Ghosts can be mixed with both front and back projections from slide or film material. Completely white relief models can be made, upon which coloured data is projected – even for subjects as complex as maps. Translucent models can be made. Glass-reinforced plastic (**GRP**) is translucent, for example, where one set of information is apparent when the model is back lit and another when it is front lit. The final stage in a diorama, the flat artwork at the rear, can be back projected and then changed, using **cross-fade** slides or film. Changing or **running titles** can be introduced. Planned, computer-controlled sequences can be used and operated by the visitor. The permutations are endless.

Mirrors

Semi-silvered mirror has been discussed at length, but ordinary mirror has a great part to play in the exhibition environment. It can be used to enlarge a seemingly narrow space; by placing mirrors strategically they can create an effect of spaciousness and continuance where none exists. Used in models, they can have the same effect; half-ship models, where a mirror reflects the other half, used to be commonplace. An enclosed landscape model will look 'boxed in', but when slim mirrors are placed at each end the model will seem to continue, again giving a feeling of length where none exists. They can be used on ceilings, subject to safety regulations (mirror plastic is available), to give an impression of height; on structures to give the impression that the supported load floats; and on floors, adequately protected by subtle barriers, to give the effect that a column or tower grows out from below the floor. They can be used under water, behind flowers, beside curtains, at the back of recesses. Mirrors used in these ways, decoratively but with practical considerations or illusion in mind, are again an area where the designer's ingenuity will always find new uses. This book cannot teach people how to design; all it can do is to open doors

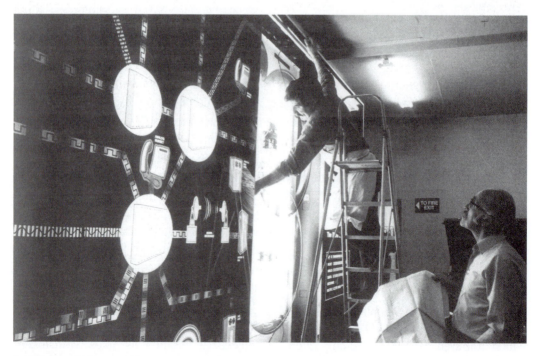

Back-lit Polaroid discs and film are rotated against each other to produce the effect of movement in a flat display. Technical Animations Ltd©.

to ideas for solutions to design problems.

Mirrors used completely for practical purposes also have a place. Where distances immediately behind a rear projection screen are too confined, the projected beam can be lengthened by the use of front silvered mirrors, but remember that every time the image passes through a mirror, it is reversed and somewhat degraded.

Other special effects

There are one or two other special effects that come into this area of solid or quasi-solid images. The first is a development of **polaroid**, where the qualities of polaroid film are exploited to produce **moiré** patterns which simulate movement on flat diagrams. Discs of polaroid are revolved behind static cut-out polaroid patterns, set into black and white on coloured film. With a light source behind them, an effect is produced where, for example, in a diagram showing the flow of fuel through an engine, the fuel seems to flow. Another

Rainbow/Benton transmission hologram commissioned by British Gas for the British Gas flotation.

patented device is the '**talking head**'. This is, in the author's opinion, a sinister device, best only for demonstrations in the Chamber of Horrors. A completely static mask is sculpted in white relief and on to it is projected generally a well-known person explaining some phenomenon or other. As the relief model is completely static, and as the talker's head has to be held in a clamp during filming, the result is macabre in the extreme, but it does seem to generate a delighted response from the very young. Another patented device, which should be popular only with the young but seems to appeal also to those of us who like practical jokes, is a televised animated cartoon face which calls out to passers-by and engages them in conversation. There is a large group of people, of whom the author is one, who would run a mile rather than talk to a televised cartoon, but surprisingly others exist who quite cheerfully do so. The device consists of a manually manipulated rubber drawing, which can be made to perform a number of basic facial movements. It is manipulated by an operator with a microphone, who is concealed behind a one-way transparent screen. The eventual image is videoed on to a screen.

Finally, and still in the process of development in terms of informative devices, come **holograms**. To date they have mainly been used as exhibits in their own right, rather than as informative aids. However, holograms responding to low-voltage lighting can be

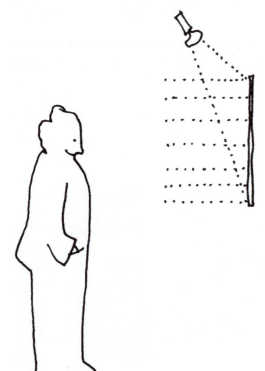

switched off to be transparent and invisible, allowing a further image to be seen beyond. At the time of writing, a hologram can be made by special photography and it is now possible to produce one digitally on a television monitor. They used to be static, but can now be mobile and computer generated. A hologram is a clearly three-dimensional image, contained in a flat plane. In its original form it was made by splitting a pure beam of laser light from one source to give both a front and an angled view of an object at the same time, thus creating the impression of depth.

A hologram must be lit from the same angle from which it was lit when photographed. If it is not, it is simply invisible.

Projection

Projection has already been mentioned in connection with dioramas and working models, but in fact it has a far greater potential role in exhibitions. We are at a point in time where one system of projection has largely taken over from another.

Until ten or so years ago, all projection in exhibitions, either of stills or moving images, was achieved using conventional methods; that is, a bright light through translucent film. The major attendant problems with this method are twofold: the lamps burn out and the films fade, so for any exhibition the costs are high and the danger of blank information spaces imminent. Over the last few years, major museums and exhibitions have replaced the ubiquitous slide screen with television monitors showing video tapes. Conferences and major sporting events have called for the development of bigger and better television projection equipment and, in recent years, the development of the video **disc** as opposed to the video tape has produced a

'Britain Before Man', Geological Museum, 1977. Topography and geology are projected from overhead on to the white relief map.

far more refined moving image and a really first class still picture. The video wall has become commonplace, that is quite literally a wall of video screens. Flat screen technology has also now been developed almost to perfection; too expensive as yet for most domestic circumstances, plasma screens are now sharp and bright enough even for outdoor use. About ten years ago the cost of producing a video disc made such displays almost prohibitively expensive; now they can be produced on a home computer. For the ordinary exhibitor, slides with automatic changing lamps and **random access** still exist; however, **film loops** stored in **loop absorbers** and projecting continuously, which were mentioned in the first edition of this book, have now almost completely disappeared.

Television projection is now very sophisticated indeed. The quality of the image is near-perfect and can be projected on to practically anything. The major controlling factor is the **ambient light**. Daylight is the arch-enemy of the exhibition designer; it is almost completely impossible to predict and to control satisfactorily if allowed in. The best place for it is out, so where complex projections and lighting effects are required, it is vital to exclude daylight as much as possible. Assuming it is largely excluded, fascinating effects can be produced by projecting on to almost anything one cares to consider. Projection on to gauze can produce ghost effects by filming against black and mixing light levels beyond the gauze with projection on the gauze. Multiscreen projection can be set up where specially prepared programmes accompanied by sound commentaries are shown. These programmes, commonly known as A/V (audio-visual) shows are controlled by computers and have a whole industry devoted to their production. Both the hardware and the software are used for conferences and sales promotions of one sort or another. Some of the A/V shows are so sophisticatedly **pulsed** and cross-faded that they can produce the effect of movement. **Split screen** projection, where two or more moving images or a still and moving image mix are shown, is another development.

All these projections must be produced by professionals with expert knowledge. They are costly and, in an exhibition, should be shown for short, clearly stated periods – between one and eight minutes, depending on the comfort of the environment. Eight minutes is a very long time to stand watching a programme. Moreover, they should be used only in short-term exhibitions if firm maintenance arrangements have been made. Shows using huge amounts of sophisticated equipment leave a great deal to go wrong. In the museum or heritage circumstance it is always best practice to advise the visitor with a static message of how long the show is and how long the interval is. This leaves them in no doubt as to whether the equipment has broken down, or if the show will ever end before their restless child tugs them on.

Sound

It has been impossible to write thus far without the mention of sound and it is, of course, commonplace with all sorts of projection but worth considering on its own. Not all sound has to be spoken commentary. Sound effects can enhance a simple display: the sound of birds with an outdoor effect or diorama, or wind and seagulls with ships or coastal scenes. It may sound corny, and indeed it is, but corn sells a lot of products and is equally useful in selling information. Sound can be more or less localized, using directional speakers, but often a discreet spill of sound lends atmosphere and acts as an enticement to visitors to move nearer to the source. Handset telephone receivers can be used (though they are vulnerable to vandals) with **solid state** sound or sound on disc supplying the sound. The medium, like all the other specialities, is best in the hands of experts, but the designer should keep up to date with the potentials from all effects in order to communicate effectively.

Another important aspect of sound is the often expressed requirement in museums and heritage centres to collect an oral history. This is done by inviting the visitor to use a microphone within an exhibition, to record his or her own memories associated with the subject or region that the exhibition describes. The equipment for this is straightforward and commercially available; however, the circumstances should be contrived to enable the visitor to record unselfconsciously and without disturbing other visitors.

Smell

Having considered sound, smell should not be forgotten. Atmosphere has often been mentioned as conducive to learning in these peculiar environments, and smell can be used discreetly to great effect. Many odours are very evocative and can be reproduced synthetically. A **pressure pad**-operated gas cylinder producing, at nose level, a shot of an appropriate smell at a good moment can be a marvellous gimmick; gimmicks are, after all, what most of the effects are, and why not if they assist in the process of enlightenment?

Lighting

Light itself is the final piece in the jigsaw puzzle of special effects. It is a puzzle, however, that can be rearranged in countless ways. The only means of bringing order to the description of the pieces has been to separate them, but there are inevitably hundreds of different permutations awaiting invention. Light is clearly the most important of all the elements relative to effective display. It is the one thing that cannot be removed. At the same time it is possible to use it poorly and inadequately, particularly as it seems to be the area in which the least startling developments have taken place since the late 1960s. Sources of light have been honed down and become more sophisticated but they still boil down to two, generally referred to as '**tungsten**' and '**fluorescent**' (in other words, a hot bulb or a cool tube). Tungsten lamps have been tidied up and low-voltage devices developed; fluorescent tubes have been slimmed down and bent into shapes resembling light bulbs, but we are still stuck with the same two basic forms. It is, as yet, not possible to

paint on light or to bend it, to float it in space or to pulse shots of it along transparent tubes. We delight in laser shows but find it very hard to use lasers economically for display. Light awaits its 'Silicon Valley'.

Meanwhile, what have we got? Tungsten and all its derivatives: halogen, quartz and so on, all giving varying degrees of sharp, hot light with a warm effect with which, even though it is not a 'natural' light and is hard to filter into one, we are most at ease. People choose tungsten generally for living rooms, for instance. In its simplest form it is used in the ordinary 25, 40, 60 and 100 watt bulbs, but exhibitions are not normally about exhibiting lamps and lampshades. They are about using lamps effectively and not much joy can be got out of a 40 watt bulb. Essentially, the general internal lighting of a display should be **recessive** and its **external lighting**, titling and

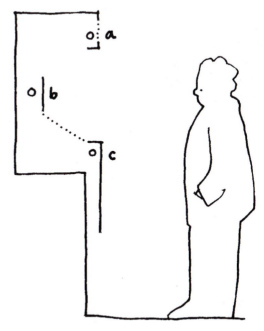

a = striplight lighting the display and back lighting a fret-cut fascia; b = striplight lighting up and down and through a transparency; c = striplight lighting the display and a skirting recess.

'Treasures of the Earth', Geological Museum, 1985. Neon (top), backlit transparency (centre) and overhead projection (bottom) all used for information and effect.

so on should be competitive. Internally, the lighting of the displays should be paramount, and frequently in an introverted exhibition the displays will emanate enough light to illuminate the exhibition, with the possible assistance of discreet **handrail**, **skirting** or **cornice** lighting to define the public spaces. Fluorescent tubes are ideal for such **linear lighting**, along with the even lighting of fascias or transparencies and the front-lighting of dioramas and models. Tungsten light is physically hot, easy to control, throws sharp shadows and can be projected over long distances. Fluorescent light is cool, comparatively hard to control, fade or turn on or off without special equipment and throws vague, fuzzy shadows. Essentially when light is used for display it should be used profusely and internally, but economically. Profusely means that there should be plenty of light. Displays

Laser light passed through glass fibres produces this dramatic effect.

ought to twinkle and cry out for attention. Internally means that the lamps should be within the confines of the display. If they are outside, they will cast shadows and cause reflections in display case glass. Economically means that as much value should be got out of each lamp as possible.

Both tungsten and fluorescent lamps cause problems for conservationists when used near valuable fabrics, paintings or prints. They both produce heat (albeit in differing quantities) and **ultraviolet** which is positively damaging to many artefacts, but most importantly they produce light. It is high numbers of lumens – measured light – that do the damage. Consult conservators before lighting precious artefacts, and consult lighting experts before embarking on extensive lighting systems.

There are other, less common, sources of light. We are all familiar with **neon**, and it is in fact very usable. It is the only source of light with which it is possible to draw, if only with stylized lines, and it can be pulsed on and off easily; hence the exotic advertisements for which it is used. It is, however, dangerous stuff using very high voltages, even when designed properly within legal constraints. It can only be manufactured to order and

British Telecom stand, Ideal Home Exhibition, 1983. Use of Perspex by the designers.

installed by experts, but it can be an excellent solution to certain problems, particularly as it can be made in a surprisingly wide range of colours using permutations of different gases and coloured tubes.

Lasers are another light source now used for projection over sometimes massive distances. Other developments will undoubtedly emerge as a by-product of some other more sophisticated, often military, requirement.

Other ways of transmitting light have been developed in recent years, one or two of them useful to the exhibition designer. **Fibre optics**, glass or plastics fibres will transmit sharp, bright light to tiny outlets some distance away from the source. This can be most useful in tiny or interactive displays. It is really useful in display lighting with very valuable exhibits, for by the time it has passed down the length of tube it is completely free of both ultraviolet and infra-red, both of which can be very damaging. The lumens are still there, though, and have to be measured. In **edge lighting**, the molecular structure of Perspex sheets allows light put in at one edge to be emitted at the other end of the sheet, possibly on an engraved line. Thus drawings engraved into glass or Perspex can be illuminated dramatically.

Perhaps the most magic source of light of them all is ultraviolet (UV), or black light, which can be used to transmit light invisibly across a space. There are UV sensitive paints and plastics (and soap powders) which respond dramatically to remote black light and provide almost a neon-like effect, but the light is not bright so it needs to be in a subdued ambiance. All these types of light and effects can and should interplay with other aspects of a display to produce really exciting results.

Interactive displays

Special effects are subject to two main types of operation: either automatic or interactive. The first means operating 'continuously and sequentially'. The second means operated by the visitor, individually or because of his or her arrival at the display. Automatic displays are easy and straightforward, but interactive displays give the visitor the chance to explore independently, and they are greatly favoured in science- or education-oriented displays in

'Man's Place in Evolution', Natural History Museum, 1980. An interactive display.

Electric cars transport the visitor through the popular part of the Jorvik exhibition in 10 minutes. The visitors then walk through the more didactic area at their own pace.

museums or interpretative centres. In these situations, the visitor's interest is generated by the display and further interest encouraged through visitor involvement. A display that responds to the visitor's arrival, participation and departure will obviously generate greater interest and, despite the sophistication of its working parts, can be of enormous value in communicating.

If the visitor is to operate an exhibit, then various methods have to be considered. There are not only buttons to press. The adjoining button is useful, though commonplace. Other impulses used are hidden; weight-sensitive pressure pads, placed underneath carpeting, respond to the visitor's presence or arrival and initiate a response, or set of responses. There are also **ultrasonic**, infra-red switches and **radar** controlled switches. Sound- and heat-sensitive switches also exist, and again we are in the area of advancing technology so further discussion of types of reaction is irrelevant except to say that if buttons are to be used they must of course be tough and durable.

The type of 'magic' response to the visitor's arrival provided by impulse methods is exactly the stuff of successful exhibitions and, when used imaginatively, can enhance the process of three-dimensional learning immensely (see Play Zone, p. 88). Other interactive displays are simply mechanical. These must be designed with the safety of the user in mind but demonstrations of engineering movement, technology, human biology, electricity, water handling, geology, and even plant growing have been contrived with which the visitor can interact in order to learn.

A very popular technique, borrowed from the ghost trains and tunnels of love of the fairground, is travel – the automated transport of the visitor through the exhibition, or of the exhibition past the visitor.

This involves using cars on tracks powered by buried cables, or giant revolves, boats in channels of moving water, pods on wires or rotating wheels and so on, all highly complex and expensive methods and only to be considered where there is money and expertise sufficient to develop the techniques, for there is no 'standard' model. There are examples of these in the Western world, and before the exhibitor or designer embarks upon this way of exhibiting it would be as well to visit such exhibitions, to find out the benefits, snags and costs. Such movement can be dramatic, exciting and fun, and when information is merged with such qualities there is a strong chance that the communication will be effective. That, of course, is what the design is all about.

Another **special effect** that emanates straight from Disneyland is **animatronics**. An animatronic figure, human, fictional or animal, is quite simply a cleverly animated figure. They can be used seated or standing, in groups or even top half or head only. They are as good as the manufacture and the message and can be similarly bad. Disney has coined the word '**imagineering**' for the design of such mechanical special effects.

But creativity cannot be taught. This chapter has presented most of the elements which can be part of a good design. It is up to the imagination of the designer to mix some, or all, of these elements effectively.

'Do's

Do remember that people's eyesight varies.

Remember:

- bifocals
- short-sighted people
- blind people and Braille
- deaf people
- short people
- tall people
- physically disabled people
- people who want to touch things.

Do remember that people have noses and ears, as well as hands and eyes.

Do remember that people need:

- to sit down
- to quench their thirst
- to go to the toilet
- to hang up their coats
- to protect their valuables.

Do remember that some people want:

- to destroy things
- to blow things up
- to steal things.

Do respect existing buildings.

'Do not's

Do not create attractive exhibits full of interest and detail that block the entrance and exit points of the exhibition.

Do not place detailed displays in such a way that a visitor looking at them will obscure other displays.

Do not design tall detailed displays. One visitor can obscure the whole thing. Orient displays laterally.

Do not put detailed information outside a band 900 mm from the floor to 2000 mm from the floor. Nobody will read it.

Do not put lights where they will blind visitors the other side of the display.

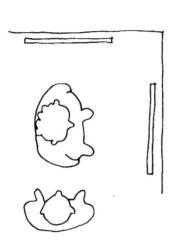

Do not put showcases with vertical glass opposite each other; this will create a hall of mirrors.

Do not force or expect people to follow a compulsory route. They will not.

Do not use long line lengths of type: 40 to 50 characters maximum.

Do not put labels in small print at the back of deep cases. Choose one size that can be read all over.

Do not site good displays in out of the way places.

Do not put labels to pictures in the shadow below them.

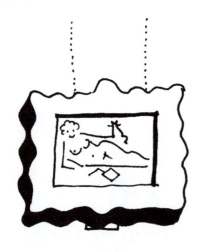

Do not put exhibits too low to be seen clearly.

Do not use handwriting.

Do not make people queue.

Do not condescend to the visitor.

Do not even consider an exhibition if there are no objects.

Do not design an exhibition if a film, book, leaflet or the Internet would do the job more satisfactorily.

Do not show off.

What is _Taste_?

Taste is one of the processes we use to make judgements about design.
The body of information we draw upon in making these judgements has accumulated across the centuries. This exhibition aims to show how this accumulation took place.
But the process is not finite: it continues today. Humans have traditional purposes and evolving needs: the process of Taste has to serve both.
The present moment is one of great diversity in matters of Taste. In revealing some of the important influences in the history of Taste this exhibition is intended to help us understand more clearly why we value certain values in design; if we can know what influences us today then perhaps we can more effectively decide what we want tomorrow.
The concept of Taste evolved when at one moment in the past there was such diversity that it was necessary to make a clear statement about what constituted the "good" in design. "Good" design and "good" taste are not necessarily the same thing: Taste is not the whole of design because it ignores function and finance, but it is the most human, immediate and evocative part of it. An exhibition about Taste is an exhibition about values in design ...

8 The design

HAVING defined the circumstances, the people, the tools and techniques, it is the time for creativity to take a bow. If genius is 1 per cent inspiration and 99 per cent perspiration, then so is creativity. Throughout all areas of design there is a point when everything narrows down, as in an hourglass. This is the point at which either very hard work or the one almost indefinable element of creativity comes into play.

The very hard work is easy enough to define and was largely covered in previous chapters. It involves the careful setting out of all the now known elements of the problem in the form of scale representations, even models of the site, the objects to be displayed, photographs, written descriptions and the designer's own notes. After this comes the sheer industry of juggling all these elements together with one's understanding of techniques and space until finally they make some kind of sense. Eventually a logical form emerges which answers all the demands and the whole concept can be put together for assessment, further tweaking and eventually presentation to colleagues and the client.

Creativity is harder to define. Psychologists, psychiatrists and academics of all sorts have been defining it for years, but one is never quite sure that they have got it right.

The author has been a designer all his professional life, but it is still impossible to say what goes on in the brain between the assimilation of all the aspects of the problem and the solution that emerges. One thing is for sure: if there is a flash of inspiration it takes place in a part of the brain to which we do not seem to have conscious access. Once it has taken place we can rationalize it, demonstrate it, and eventually execute it. But that point – that particular narrowing of the hourglass – is not a conscious moment.

Many a designer confronted with a clear description of a problem will do a sketch on a scrap of paper. That first piece of visual evidence is the sole tangible representative of a subconscious creative moment, and it is that moment of sharply focused creativity which is inspiration. The artist James McNeill Whistler, when asked how he dared to demand as much as two guineas for a mere two hour's work, replied that he asked it for the knowledge of a lifetime.

There are dangers associated with the creative process as well as many external enemies. The client who comes to the designer with preconceived notions of the solution will stultify design; the client who expects an invention from the designer when he has produced no brief at all is asking for the impossible. The designer who expects the client to accept his intuitive solution at face value is asking for trouble, and this is where post-rationalization comes in. No matter how confident the designer is of the value or rightness of his solution, he must justify it intellectually. This sometimes means trudging back through the brief with the solution in mind, making sure that it works on every front, testing it in fact against every eventuality. If this is done away from the client, then the designer is in a far better position to 'sell' the idea to the client than if he or she wanders in and airily announces that this is what we are going to do. The client, who might well be wary of intuition, needs to see that a thoughtful process has taken place. Consequently, if the designer produces the design there and then at the first meeting without any apparent effort, he is obviously asking for trouble.

Another danger is the client who is over-eager to be a part of the creative process and pours out ideas which are generally out of date and inappropriate. This type of client has to be dealt with very carefully, and the successful designer will spend quite a lot of time reassuring the client of the value of their suggestions while demonstrating gently their impossibility. Diplomatic stuff. If the designer is concerned to give the public something of real value, then it is not a device to be ashamed of.

Although Chapter 3 discusses the client, this seems a more appropriate place to discuss such problems. Another problem is that there seems to be confusion in the non-designer's mind between designers and inventors. Some inventors are acclaimed as designers because their inventions are attractive to look at as well as functional – the Dyson vacuum cleaner for example. They are not designers in the sense we are discussing. Designers respond to a brief issued by others. It may be a poor brief and need adjusting by the designer, but the initiator of the idea was the client. The designer responds to that brief with his skills, techniques and tools together with his experience, and produces a creative or inventive design. It is very important to remember that exhibition designers are communicators; our role is therefore not as composers but as interpreters, in the same way as instrumentalists are and, like them, our interpretations are at best creative and inspired.

If in the context of problem solving you have never experienced a flash of inspiration, then do not despair. We are all creative, but creativity needs nourishing. In the case of the designer it is nourished by knowledge and experience. The hard work that has been mentioned earlier is the nursery school for creativity – the same is true of anyone choosing a career that involves responding to the requirements, demands or needs of others.

Design presentation

That hard work, that flash of inspiration, that sketch or scribble has now to be transformed into a huge three-dimensional thing of sometimes enormous complexity. The design has to travel from the designer's mind to the myriad of other professionals who are going to make the exhibition possible. This journey, starting with the sketch and ending with a precise set of drawings and specifications, is also the subject of this chapter.

After all the creative work, the assembling of the information and the objects, and after the discussions involved – the ideas, proposals and rejected schemes – comes the practical side: the actual construction of the exhibition. For some people this is the most exciting part of the process; for others it is simply a procedural necessity after the stimulating early stages. In any event it is essential and, while many of these processes are devolved from the design and management in to the hands of specialists, constant supervision is required throughout. This supervision is not because the specialists are inadequate or inexperienced, but because the communication of complex and often original ideas from the designer to the maker is a difficult and sometimes unsatisfactory process. Here a series of face-to-face explanations, briefing and ongoing consultation is frequently the best method.

The primary means of communicating the design to manufacturers is by drawings. There are two types: accurate 'scale' drawings and visuals or **perspectives**, sometimes called '**artist's impressions**' which show what the finished product should look like. The visuals are useful to give an idea of the appearance of the end product, but the scale drawings are essential. A scale drawing is an accurate plan with **elevations** (side views) and **sections** (cuts through) nowadays generally done using Computer Aided Design (**CAD**) but sometimes drawn neatly in ink or pencil on to paper. Scale in this context means that on the drawings, one centimetre might represent one metre. This is shown as 1:100, or an inch might represent one foot, shown as 1" to 1'0". There are many variations on these scales, but clearly all drawings should either be done in the metric or **duodecimal** system. A small-scale metric drawing to show whole plans and elevation will be 1:100 and a small scale duodecimal drawing will be 1/8" to 1'0". For normal purposes

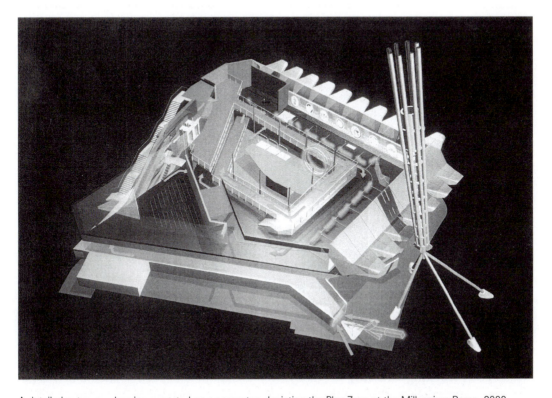

A detailed cut-away drawing executed on a computer, depicting the Play Zone at the Millennium Dome, 2000.

An 'artist's impression' or visual, created entirely on a computer, depicting the Play Zone at the Millennium Dome, 2000.

section details of construction, showcases, handrails, stairs and so on might be drawn to a large scale at 1:5 metric or 3" to 1'0" (quarter full-size) duodecimal.

With CAD in common use, it is now possible to produce accurate visuals of both the interior and the exterior of any proposed scheme almost at the press of a button or two on a keyboard.

It is also possible to produce animations or 'walks through' of any scheme, great or small. All this constantly changing and evolving technology is very exciting, useful and impressive, but two things should never be forgotten. First, the ability to draw freehand is an invaluable tool for a designer at meetings and among colleagues for expressing ideas; drawing itself is a marvellous aid to observation and understanding. If one lets a computer do all the work the personal evolution of a designer will be inevitably slowed down. Second, computer-drawn perspectives, while being extraordinarily accurate, can have a sterile quality. There is no human touch, and as a result they can be less effective in the process of communicating ideas and personality. Visuals are obviously useful both as presentation aids and as guides to contractors and craftspeople.

A multiplicity of copies of all types of drawing is required for estimating, subcontracting and construction stages. Today copying is cheap and commonplace, and more or less **true to scale** (TTS). Since all papers shrink and expand slightly, depending on humidity and climate, important dimensions should always be written on to drawings as well as being drawn as accurately as possible.

A good **working drawing** is orderly, well laid out and explicit. It should be read at best from left to right and from top to bottom. If the plan, sections and elevations are on

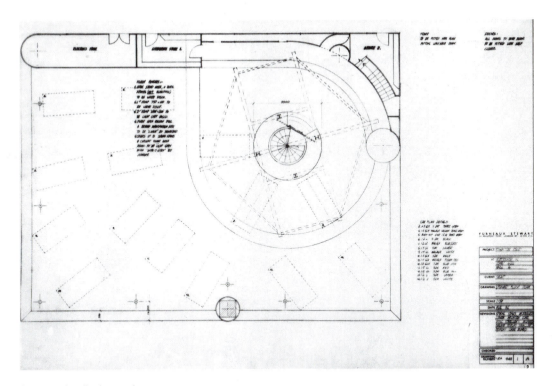

A conventionally drawn plan.

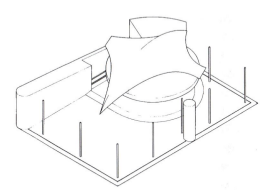

A visual of the same exhibition stand.

The finished article.

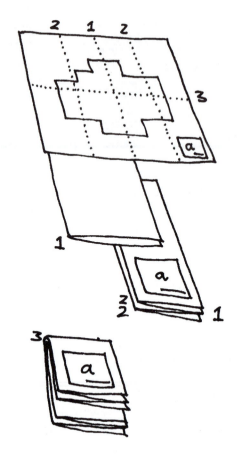

The correct way to fold a drawing: fold 1 on to itself, in half; fold 2 each half back to expose drawing title 'a'; fold 3 in half lengthwise, title 'a' still exposed.

one sheet, then the plan should be at the bottom, with elevations over it and sections to the right. The plan should have the sides from where the elevations are 'viewed' clearly marked, along with the 'cut' lines of the sections. All the text on the drawings should be computer-driven, written clearly in a good hand, or applied in **stencilled** lettering. Wherever possible, this lettering should be horizontal; sometimes, however, dimensions are shown running along the line, so a height would involve vertical writing, which should always point in the same direction. The best drawings contain all the relevant information including the code numbers of other drawings upon which large-scale details can be found. It is worth remembering that these drawings are read by many different people. The name of the design organization, together with project designer, draughtsperson and appropriate telephone numbers, street or e-mail addresses should be on the drawing, preferably placed in a box set in the bottom right hand corner where it can easily be found. Drawings should never be rolled, always folded. Rolled drawings can become unmanageable and the user will become enmeshed in a quire of rolls from which he may never emerge.

The correct way to fold a drawing is so that it lies flat for the user when unfolded and reveals the title and the design firm's name when folded up.

The first destination of the working drawing is the contractor's office. Exhibition contractors exist as specialist organizations. If they cannot be traced locally, then many **shopfitting** firms undertake the same work. Firms are often specialists in both. Sometimes the 'small works' division of a building contractor will undertake exhibition work. Both permanent and temporary exhibitions are specialist work. A great deal of quick thinking is required from all involved, from the contractor's representative, through to the **workshop** manager, the estimator and the craftspeople – carpenters, painters and sign-writers on the shop floor. The carpenters are in fact a special breed, often despised by their more conventional fellows because they are always willing to attempt anything: to cut corners, to solve problems in a way that is not at all 'by the book' in order to achieve some special finish or detail. The mixture of woodworking and display demands a certain delicacy of touch, a sensitivity, a lateral thinker who is constrained neither by training nor by set solutions. The same is true of all craftspeople in the field, who are frequently asked to take either personal or professional risks to solve the problems that arise.

The very fact of deadlines adds to the instant nature of the work; the show must open on time. Occasionally, even after the most careful planning, '**ghosters**' (all night work) must be done to complete on time, and despite the difficulty the camaraderie developed under circumstances like this is often rewarding and memorable. At best it is a very stimulating business where management, designers and craftspeople are equal in their efforts to obtain the best results.

The estimator

The person who brings together any contractor with any designer is essentially the estimator, for it is the competitive price that wins the **contract**. The estimator is a specialist who goes over the drawings millimetre by millimetre, costing out everything to be used in the construction. To this end a certain amount of written information will be helpful. This can be either, as has been said, on the drawing or separately, in the form of a specification. The former method has the advantage that all the information is to hand for both the estimator and the maker, but it is quite common and satisfactory for a separate, typed, detailed specification to be done for reading in conjunction with the drawings. The estimator will literally price every nail, screw or piece of wallpaper to be used in the construction. In addition to an estimation of the time it will take to build and transport it, together with subsistence, contingencies and profit, this will constitute the price the contractor submits to his potential client. Most estimating is done in competition with other contractors to the client's price advantage, but it is only possible to compete fairly when identical drawings, specifications and estimating time are given to each competitor.

When **estimates** are required from individual specialists, artists or model-makers, it is impossible to go in for competitive tendering. The input from each craftsperson will be different and the briefing will differ from one individual to another, depending upon the ideas thrown up at the time. It is a good idea under these circumstances to select a craftsperson who will best respond to a particular problem, and either ask for an estimate of the cost of the agreed solution or to allocate a certain sum within which to work. This is of course an area where experience and knowledge of a wide range of specialists is invaluable. No matter what, both sorts of contractor need good working drawings. They serve to define clearly the space within which the specialist is to work. The second major use of working drawings is actually to construct the exhibition.

It is worth pointing out that some design practices lean more heavily on the contractor's drawing office than others. If great reliance is placed upon the contractor two things must be considered: the contractor will rightly charge more for his work, and the designer should be prepared to supervise such **detailed** drawing work very closely if he wants to get the effects he has in mind.

No matter which process, the drawings go first to the works manager, who will be briefed by the estimator and if possible the designer, to ensure that there are no misunderstandings and to effect any changes that the estimator might have recommended. The job supervisor, usually an experienced craftsperson, will also suggest changes and short-cuts, and these must be discussed. From manager and supervisor, the drawings will go to a '**setter out**'. This is a draughtsperson who will draw up everything to full size on huge sheets of paper. These are sometimes called '**rods**' after the lengths of wood that used to be marked up to show accurate running dimensions for use in workshops or building sites. These rods are used by the carpenters who can measure off at full size the work they have to do. In many contractors' premises there are cutting workshops, where all the timbers or boards are cut to size and then delivered to the joiners. A big job will be given a supervisor at this stage and a team of carpenters, who will generally stay with the job from the shop floor to the exhibition site. A good designer will take an interest at all these stages and get to know the supervisor and the team. Good relationships and a respect for the craftspeople's skills will lead far more surely to a good finished product than absentee dictation of requirements. The contractor's workshop, if you are encouraged to visit (and you only will be if you behave properly in it, is fascinating.

Systems

Another method of construction entails the use of systems. These are prefabricated units, like LEGO, which can be bought or hired and assembled in a number of different ways. Many systems come with a miniature kit which can be used to assist the design process. The amount of creativity and true design work involved when using a system is clearly very much less than when starting from scratch, but it is not to be scorned unless it is misused; for example, either specified by a non-designer to avoid using a designer, or used by a designer as a lazy solution to a problem. Their main use is for shell schemes or for exhibition stands which need to be erected and dismantled several times. They are also abused when they are considered simply as vehicles for graphic displays with no consideration given to planning or circulation. There are of course systems which are better than others, which naturally cannot be quoted here, but the best of them offer the widest possible versatility for the least amount of expenditure. The best systems are also recessive in character and do not proclaim their origins; exhibitions are, after all, for selling goods other than systems. The oldest system is the stock panel, generally 2400 x 1200 X 50 mm ply on batten, used over and over again for shell schemes or straightforward exhibition walls.

Contractors

Not only do the carpenters turn flat drawings into three-dimensional structures, but the electricians are doing early off-site wiring of light boxes and so on, and the painters are undercoating or spray finishing special units. The artwork shop is preparing full size layouts for cut-out lettering and finally, if double-deckers or metal structures are involved, the metalwork is taking shape in the metal shop.

A contractor's workshop is no place for the clumsy, the insensitive or the garrulous, so visits should be carefully planned and arranged to be of maximum value to the progress of the job and the least inconvenient to the contractor. The same is true of visits to the specialist craftsperson. Every minute is money within the tight profit margins of small companies; posses of grey-suited designers, managers and clients taking up space in the middle of a workshop are not welcome unless strictly needed.

A typical exhibition contractor's workshop: C-Beck Limited, Chessington, Surrey.

Sub-contractors

Some exhibition contractors sub-contract certain bits of work. This is entirely up to them, though there are a limited number of specialist sub-contractors. In time, most designers get to know those in their area quite well. The main tasks to be sub-contracted are electrical and metalwork, photographic enlargements, **screen printing** and sometimes painting and decorating.

The main contractor will often have a regular association with the sub-contractors and will simply ask them for a price, but occasionally will go out to **tender**. To this end, further copies of drawings may be requested, specifically marked up or highlighted for perhaps electrical work or decorative finishes. This marking up is done in one of two ways. The first method is by having a second copy made; new details can then be added to this and more copies made. The second method, on perhaps a less complex job, is to mark on to a new copy with coloured felt pens the extra information. In either of these ways, electrical, decorative or special effects mark-ups can be produced for distribution. Obviously the latter type are less easily reproduced, and are generally made only after a contract has been let to clarify work for the single successful contractor.

The sub-contractors will be supervised by the main contractor, and requests for changes or expressions of concern about their work should always go through the main contractor – partly out of simple politeness, but also to avoid confusion.

Specialist contractors

Special-effects contractors are generally supervised by the designers or production managers and, when there is one, the supplier of the technical information that the special effect is intended to communicate. It is essential that they should supervise together, the designer because of the interpretative and constructional elements, the specialist to ensure that the effect accurately represents the science, technology or historical facts involved, and the manager to ensure that there is no extra cost involved.

Away from major cities, it is frequently difficult to find special-effects makers. The author is frequently asked where to find such people. It should never be impossible. Model making, for instance, is a more or less common profession; the **Yellow Pages** or the electronic version on the Internet will have a section for them, but enquiries among architects or surveyors should elicit some names of model makers. They often have, or can quickly acquire, other skills such as diorama making. Some are good at exact representations from architects' or engineers' drawings; others show strengths with figures, animals or vegetation. Taxidermists can also be found through the *Yellow Pages*, local natural history societies or museums.

There are craftspeople who specialize in plastics or metals. There are carpenters who specialize in pattern making. These can often be tracked down through suppliers of basic materials. Visits to model making or hobby shops can prove profitable, as the shopkeepers are invariably knowledgeable and helpful, and often experts themselves in one field or another. There are craftspeople who specialize in cut-away models or artefacts, or cut-away drawings. Most car manufacturers or consumer durable manufacturers need **prototypes**, instruction leaflets or training manuals and photographs for publicity, and generally will be delighted to pass on names, particularly if their company name will appear with a grateful acknowledgement in the **credits** for the exhibition.

Sculptors and artists, unless very well established, are generally willing to take on commissioned work. If models of people or animals are needed, or murals or **backdrops**, then approaches to local arts societies can often prove profitable. Again, the *Yellow Pages* under 'artists' agents' could be useful.

Some of the finest landscape models are made for **flight simulators** in the aircraft industry and are frequently associated with considerable electronic ingenuity. Aircraft companies or airlines should be able to provide information on the specialists they use. Some of the most sophisticated, yet commonplace, electronics are found in the world of computers and television, video and sound reproduction and cameras; again, shopkeepers themselves may know of specialists.

Pursuing lines of enquiry, starting at the simplest level, can prove rewarding and interesting. If computer drawing or graphics is required this is now commonplace; the sophistication of these devices rises in direct proportion to the rate at which the costs –

A flight simulator. Inside: apparent reality . . .

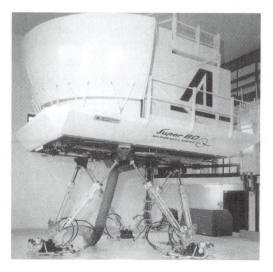

. . . outside: the truth. All of the expertise and technology that was used to produce these very expensive simulators could also be used on a much smaller scale for special effects in exhibitions.

and therefore availability – drop. Today's magic is tomorrow's standard equipment, and the space between today and tomorrow is shrinking all the time.

Advertising agencies are another good source of information on models or animators; often one sees a commercial containing a technique or style exactly suited to solving a particular problem. But be careful: animated film, and indeed all **purpose-made** film, is an expensive solution to a communication problem. Graphic designers and illustrators can be traced through advertisers or publishing companies. Keep a lookout for styles or gimmicks that are suitable for certain solutions, and always make a note of anything that might be useful one day and track it down there and then.

Always look at the work of any specialist with an eye to the possible application of it, or the materials involved, to your needs. The dentist makes accurate, fast, moulded reproductions. Out of what? Where do the blacksmith, the watchmaker, the imaginative car mechanic exist? Who makes that button or machine, the engraved plate on that engine, that back-lit instruction panel, that video game in a motorway café? No matter what, special-effects makers are made and not born. They evolve through accidental meetings and bizarre requests into geniuses who can make anything from a space ship for a film to a fossil tree texture in GRP to clad an exhibition showcase.

Site construction

Once all the parts of an exhibition that can be made in a workshop have been completed, then, dates permitting, work on site can commence. In a commercial exhibition this is generally a matter of days, but even in an exhibition in a special venue or a museum, work away from the workshop always costs more; therefore site work is best kept to a minimum. The first thing to get right in a commercial venue is the orientation of the stand. On island sites this can prove to be a problem; they have been known to be built the wrong way round. The designer should check, if there is a shadow of doubt, by visiting the site on the first morning of the build-up. Once checked, then any electrical **conduiting** can be laid in or services tapped before the platform is built (usually 100 mm high). Most major structures have platforms; lesser shell scheme stands or booths rarely do. The platform generally consists of 80 mm × 50 mm **unplaned** timbers on edge with a 20 mm board covering. On top of this flat finish, a carpet or special floor finish is laid early on and then protected with heavy duty polythene stapled over it until opening day. Cutting carpet or PVC around complex exhibits is time consuming and eventually wasteful; as a quantity of exhibition carpet is re-used, it is best to build the exhibition over it. This does not apply in museums, where it is rare to have a platform. Usually a carpet or special finish is laid directly on to the floor.

If a museum building is an old or converted one and the architects were not aware of the specific needs of museum exhibits, this often means that all services have to be brought in at high level, which is an important consideration at the design stage. It should also be remembered that for permanent structures, in public buildings, there are sets of safety standards somewhat different from those permitted for a short time on an exhibition site. When specifying for such work, it should be made clear on drawings and specifications that such local or national rules should be respected by main and sub-contractors. Some design organizations have a specially printed label made to this effect, for use on all drawings. This ensures that the responsibility lies with the contractor and, in the event of default, the blame will be correctly apportioned since the designer cannot possibly check in detail all the joints made, materials used and fireproofing activities undertaken.

If the exhibition is a trade fair booth or stall, then the walls and a rudimentary floor covering will have been provided. For a professional-looking job, the generally cheap-looking floor covering should be jettisoned, or the organizers should have been asked to omit it. It is possible to put up a good-looking stand within a shell scheme, and it is generally worth it, but only if a completely new structure is erected within it. The organizers' permission must be obtained and their rules adhered to, but it is still possible, and the end result will stand out from its surroundings: the main aim!

If metalwork is required for a double-decker structure, this is often the first part to be put down; sometimes before the platform if the load needs to be spread. In this case the entire area beneath the board covering to the platform should be laid with stout timbers, upon which the steel-work can be placed and bolted. Once the platform is in place and carpeted, and the metal work complete, the carpenters can be let loose to construct the exhibition. At this stage, site visits become important but they should be discreet and short. Work should not be delayed in those deadline circumstances by either chat or an absent designer who is needed to explain confusing drawings or changes in detailing. Design or management should maintain a regular but low profile on site, discreetly checking all details, answering questions and commissioning in writing **extras** that are absolutely necessary. On-site extras are a costly business, first because site time is expensive and second, with a designer's mistake, rectification is absolutely necessary, so it will not be cheap. The answer is not to make mistakes. If the contractor makes a mistake, he will pay for it.

Once the bulk of the joinery work is done, the painters will arrive. However, normally in the organized rush, painters, carpenters and electricians will work around each other with the painter doing essential tidying up after holes have been made for the electrician. They should all be attended by a labourer or two on site to clean up continually, as accidents happen in messy circumstances. People working to meet a deadline can trip over flexes covered by wood shavings perhaps, and serious injuries may ensue.

There is a peculiar feature about contractors working on temporary exhibitions: everything is hired. This means in fact that every part of the exhibition, although made to the designer's specifications, remains the property of the builder. Peculiar shapes or cases are generally scrapped at the end of the show, but stock wall panels can be retained, as can platforms, carpets, fascia boards, beams or metalwork. Some of it goes for scrap, but electrical fittings are always kept: lamps, tubes, plug sockets and tops can all be re-used. This hire procedure actually reduces costs for the client and probably started in order to ensure that the contractor turned up at the end of the show to clear away the exhibit. Obviously it does not apply to permanent work or, indeed, if the client wishes to buy a special feature, in which case arrangements can be made with the contractor.

Hiring applies elsewhere. All standard furniture can be selected from catalogues of firms accredited by the organizers; to buy items for short periods is clearly absurd. There are firms specializing in the hire of plants and flowers and their attendant accessories; the firm will also maintain the plants during the course of the exhibition.

At the appropriate time the exhibits, special effects, models and so on are delivered to the site. The designer or manager and client representative should supervise their unloading and delivery to the stand, their unpacking and their installation. If there are valuable exhibits, this is the time that security guards arrive. With valuable and/or fragile exhibits, the specialists should be the people to unpack them and to attend to their installation and display. As can be imagined, by now the site is buzzing with activity: craftspeople of all kinds, special effects people, specialists, security officers, design and management. If possible, the commissioning clients must be kept away: unless they are very experienced and relaxed they will almost certainly be in a state of panic, concerned that the show will not open on time – 'How can all this mess be cleared up by tomorrow?', 'Where is this one to be displayed?' The best place for them is in their own office, available in case of disaster or essential change.

It is, however, an expensive time for change. Design, as has been shown, involves thinking something through as a whole enterprise, planning it carefully, drawing it accurately and supervising it closely through workshops and studios. To feel constrained to change things on site is a sign, first that this process has not been as thorough as it should have been, and second that the designer (and this is serious) is not capable of the careful forethought necessary. Assuming he or she is thorough and capable, then a desire to change is simply a demonstration of insecurity and lack of confidence, and should be resisted for it will almost inevitably be a mistake. In fact, the exhibition will never look right until it is complete; since it was conceived as a whole, it must emerge as a whole before being assessed. Then, and only then, absolutely essential fine adjustments can be made.

In all these circumstances the client is best elsewhere. He or she, neither trained nor experienced in visualizing, is likely to turn up on site, notice innumerable unfinished details and then hare around telling everyone – who already knows – what needs fixing, painting or hiding. It is to be hoped that no actual or potential 'client' will be offended, reading this – no accusation of incompetence is intended.

Just as the client is a fish out of water in the moments before the exhibition is complete, so the designer is superfluous once the exhibition is open. The only real work now for the designer is to take care, particularly on a permanent exhibition, of any **snags** or defects that have emerged. This is best done with the production manager, and off site and out of sight.

9 The production

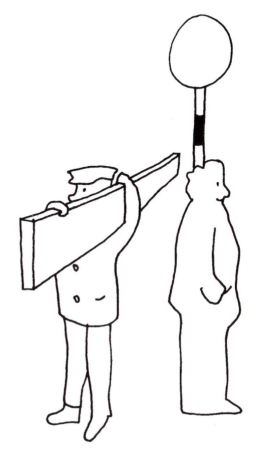

ANY enterprise involving more than one person has to be managed; even lifting a plank can be hazardous if there is no co-ordination. If the plank has to be made, purchased, delivered, used and eventually disposed of within an ordained sum of money and time-frame, then clearly a certain amount of expertise is required. Needless to say, even the simplest exhibition is a little more complex than a plank. Production management is therefore essential if it is to be executed successfully. A designer must appreciate the need for such management as a separate field of expertise, even if he or she is a 'good manager'. If this is not appreciated, and the designer attempts to manage as well as design the project, time-consuming details will distract attention from the considerable demands of design already discussed, to the detriment of any project.

Production management should not be considered a lesser profession than design; it is simply a different specialization within the same industry. As things stand most contemporary **production managers** or companies have evolved, training up staff as they went along, but just as with designers it is very important that they should be specifically experienced in exhibition production. As will have been seen, exhibitions are too specialist, too complex perhaps to be led by partnerships or companies dabbling in the business for fun or extra profit.

There is no reason why an exhibition production manager should not head up a production team which might include the designer – in fact, it can be as well if one does. Using management skills to protect the creative part of the team in order to get the best out of it makes a lot of sense. Good production management is a smooth, efficient, creative process adding enormously to the value of the end product; the worst kind of management, generally in the hands of amateurs or non-specialists, is uncaring, obstructive, prescriptive, unyielding, bossy, interfering and ignorant.

Good exhibition design managers are hard to come by, largely because there is no specific training for them. But an exhibition production manager is effectively a producer handling creative, practical and technical aspects in the one role. The **project manager** or producer therefore plans, organizes and manages tasks and resources to accomplish a defined objective within constraints of time and cost. They will programme the design process with the design and consultant team to ensure that the design information described in the previous chapter gets to the contractors in good time. They then monitor the construction on and off site.

The best background for a production manager is probably contractual. The successful manager might well have spent some early years in an exhibition or shopfitting works, moving from section to section learning the processes involved, or from one contracting firm to another, seeking experience and advancement. Early days might have been spent as a tea-boy, carpenter's mate, management trainee, draughtsperson or an apprentice estimator. No matter what, production experience and a fair, if general, grounding in costing and financial matters along with contracts, transport and site work is fundamental.

If a student on a design course shows a weakness in creative skills but demonstrates organizational strengths, then management might well be a good course for that person to follow after graduation. Junior work in a design office, with a strong emphasis on management and production problems, could make a good basis upon which to build a career. It must be emphasized, however, that while exhibition management is without specialist training, general management skills and of course skills such as accountancy can be taught and there are many specialist degree, postgraduate and diploma courses. Such training, combined with realistic practical experience in the exhibition industry, could well produce a very effective manager.

There are several production management organizations, but it is obviously best to describe an ideal. In many ways the more eclectic the mix of experience the better. Exhibitions of all kinds demand, as has been shown earlier, ever expanding skill sets and the more first-hand experience the producer can call upon the better. One such established production company has within its organization staff members culled from the theatre, architecture, commercial exhibitions, the building industry, museums, design management, business studies and the club circuit. The simple though significant benefit of such a mix means that they can introduce key personnel at different phases of a large project whilst offering an internal cross-fertilization of minds within the company.

There is a practical side to most designers' work, which should enable a designer to appreciate the need for management and organization. This chapter is devoted to describing aspects of good management which will, it is hoped, assist in the relationship between design and management, with the aim of producing first-rate large or small exhibitions for the client and of course the visitor.

The ideal production manager will be flexible and able to relate equally to suppliers, designers, contractors and clients. He or she must not be easily manipulated and will need to be tough but good mannered. An understanding of the necessity for production and financial control and constraints is essential, as is respect for and understanding of designers and the need for design.

Overseas exhibitions

We should nod in the direction of overseas exhibitions at this point. They fall into two general categories: those planned in the home country and constructed abroad, and those planned and constructed in the home country and erected by home contractors on a foreign site. The former should really only apply to the simplest possible constructions such as shell schemes; there are too many accidents possible if there is anything complex involved. Not all countries have the same or similar organizations for exhibition production, so if any foreign venture is envisaged then a preliminary visit is essential to establish lines of communication. In the second category, shipping clearly becomes a major consideration, weight and size obviously affecting cost, and shipping time obviously affecting any **production schedule**. There are professional shipping agencies in most countries, and they should be consulted at the outset. There can also be problems with foreign labour on foreign soil. These vary from country to country, and embassy officials (**Commercial Attachés**) ought to know the answers, and ought to be consulted.

Planning and resources

Because management is essential, chronological and procedural, it would be best to present the management involvement using a **production chart**. These pages are neither big enough nor suitable to show such a chart, but by using a simple flow-chart as a guide the processes can be explained.

As was mentioned earlier, exhibitions come in all shapes and sizes. For the sake of this chapter we will consider exhibitions ranging from the *super colossal* – the Millennium Dome for example, effectively a major government initiative – to the *small*, an exhibition in a shell scheme built by others or a portable display for a library or museum entrance. In between will come a *major project* such as a world fair or a large new museum; a *large project* such as the central feature of the Ideal Home exhibition perhaps or a new heritage centre; a *medium project* such as a large stand for a manufacturer at the motor show or a new gallery in a museum. So we have in mind the super colossal, the major, the large, the medium and the small.

These categories can only serve as a rough guide. There is room for great variety within them, therefore the timing, staff and general resources allocated to each phase of a project will vary enormously. The resources for a medium-size project are shown on the following diagram.

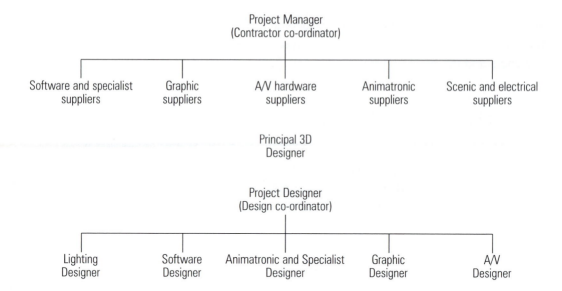

Tasks and timing

Now that the personnel are established it is necessary to look at tasks and timing. Assuming that the horizontal element of a production chart will be entirely involved with timing and progress, the vertical element on the left of the chart will be devoted to tasks; the tasks on the same medium-size project whose resources are shown above are divided into key areas, and they are as follows:

1 **concept design**
2 concept brief
3 concept design
4 client presentation, response and approval
5 **scheme design**
6 schematic design
7 client presentation, response and approval
8 **detail design**
9 detail design period
10 client presentation, response and approval
11 **financial**
12 budget parameters established
13 costs apportioned and assembled
14 quotes obtained
15 costs finalized

Ulster '71. The largest exhibition of its type since the Festival of Britain. It was produced in 18 months by a team consisting of a project leader-cum-script writer, two managers, two 3D designers and a graphic designer. The erection was supervised on site in Belfast by a member of the production team.

16   orders finalized
17   **3D implementation**
18   off-site fabrication
19   access to site permitted
20   construction on site
21   animatronic fit out
22   **venues**
23   provisional example listing issued
24   approval of exhibition/venue feasibility
25   **animatronic/specimen detail**
26   provisional listing issued
27   confirmed listing issued
28   animatronic technical details confirmed
29   **scripting and graphics**
30   content script from client
31   graphic content developed
32   client presentation, response and approval
33   detailed graphic development
34   client presentation and approval
35   final script and images from client*
36   artworking
37   client copywriting
38   client presentation, response and approval
39   artwork signed off**
40   production and installation
41   **commissioning**
42   3D snagging
43   lighting animatronic programming
44   final levels set, and clean
45   press opening

Quite a lot! Needless to say, on another project the key elements could include A/V, inter-active exhibits, working models and indeed everything that was described in Chapter 7.

---

*   It is important to remember that particularly in the case of museum exhibitions the final script is often produced by academics who are not necessarily used to tight schedules; it can therefore become the longest lead item on any schedule.

** **Signing off** means exactly that. Before any artwork is injected into the final production process it must be examined by the relevant initiator and literally signed off as being exactly right. The process of changing a piece of incorrect artwork after an exhibition of any type is complete is very costly; so the 'fault' if it does sneak in must be laid at the right door.

The above is simply a typical example but it is important to note that while designers, producers and contractors will all be very experienced, they may be working with a client who has never commissioned an exhibition before, a **'virgin' client**. Such a client will need a great deal of diplomatic hand holding and it is in that area that sensitive production management can be at its most effective.

Financial management

As with the designer, the role of the producer certainly involves creativity and indeed lateral thinking, but these attributes are often kept at a discreet distance from both the designer and the client. The producers are at their best performing their essential functions recessively. These functions include financial checks against the key areas. Financial monitoring under any circumstances, personal, commercial or public, is a sensitive area. Ongoing control must be exercised over both the designer's creative aspirations and the client's ambitions. A fixed budget is just that and therefore a vital part of the brief. To overstep it, except under exceptional circumstances, is very unprofessional.

The financial area of the producer's job would involve many checks as detailed below:

- client budget level including grey areas
- allocating the budget with the design team
- obtaining quotes
- producing a detailed budget and agreeing it with the client
- issuing orders to the contractors and agreeing progress payments
- reconciling the final costs with the agreed budget and the contingency allowance.

For the sake of this work there are a great number of generalizations and simplifications, the simplest of which is the plank with which this chapter started. However, due to the circumstances that exist at the beginning of the twenty-first century, there can be projects of enormous complexity; they could be referred to as **'sprawling' projects**. It might also be a project in need of funding (or is it simply funding in need of a project?). Such projects might be laid down through a vast array of public, governmental and other bodies who might be involved in funding a particular scheme. These in the UK could be regional, district and local councils; the Millennium Commission, various lottery boards – arts, sports and so on; English Partnerships, the Heritage Lottery Fund (HLF), European Regional Development Fund and so on. Sprawling projects often start as a gleam in a politician's or philanthropist's eye. He or she will almost inevitably be a virgin client and will flail around among the great and good culling talent from all the wrong places and funds from every source under the sun. Each talent will have an axe to grind and each source of funds will have a bureaucracy.

The financial involvement of the producer with a sprawling contract is vast, and it would be hard to imagine a production company managing such a project without members of staff who were trained in accountancy.

It must be self-evident that without all the qualities and experience mentioned above, the co-ordination of such a mish-mash of egos and ambitions would be near impossible. Without such experience the end result is very unlikely to be successful.

It is true to say, however, that no matter the project, the quality of the design team, or the sophistication of the client, production management can make or break any venture; it is as crucial as that. Good management, like good design, is not conspicuous and the modesty and maturity needed to fulfil this behind-the-scenes but vital role are difficult to develop. All design needs management, and the sooner this is recognized by all design and architectural schools, the better. At the moment, good production managers are born and evolve. The sooner it is taught as a specialization the better. If the designer on any project has to concentrate on all the aspects of production detailed in the previous pages, the creative input and attention to detail will inevitably suffer, to the detriment of the finished product.

10 The completion

THE ideal time for the client to arrive on site, even if he or she has sneaked the odd look from a distance beforehand, is just as the cleaners are **stripping off** the protective coverings from the displays. The sheets of polythene are cleared away from the carpet and wrapped exhibits; the designer is making final adjustments to the lighting, and a single painter is wandering around with a small brush and a paint pot or two, searching for missed patches or scratches to be covered. The production manager is standing, rubbing his hands and rocking back on tired feet and calf muscles, and the project designer – if there is one – is amiably arguing with the contractor's representative over sheaves of notes about extras. That is a good time to arrive.

The stand is emerging like a butterfly from a chrysalis and is, it is hoped, a little ahead of its neighbours; certainly better, bigger and in a more favourable position. The press are expected in a few minutes and suddenly there is the client, a trolley full of drinks and glasses behind him. A posse of well-presented company **representatives**, fresh and interested, are moving through the staff areas checking space, orientation and facilities of one sort or another; if it's a commercial exhibition, brochures and sales literature are being loaded on to counters and leaflet racks.

The client

At this point, there is only one thing the designer needs from the client: solid, undiluted, hyperbolic praise. No matter what criticisms there are (and they will emerge soon enough), at this moment emotions are running high and even the most objective criticism will be taken as a personal insult.

If the client is seriously unhappy, he or she must get together with the production manager to try to resolve the situation. Errors arising at this stage must be the result of poor communications, in which case the client and the design and production team are all at fault. The client's wishes have been wilfully ignored by the designer, or the client's dele-gate has not communicated adequately with his seniors. The solution to poor communi-cation between designer and client is compromise. The solution to wilful designer behaviour, sometimes called artistic temperament, is for the designer to be lured away from the site completely while the management sorts it out. This is obviously very bad practice and should never be allowed to happen. The solution to poor communication in the client organization is for the senior client to buy his way out of the problem, provided that there is time.

In a well-ordered world none of these calamities should come to pass. However, nobody can avoid certain problems; for example, non-deliveries because of weather or natural disasters, small slip-ups when working abroad, unavailability of a certain tool or connector, a missing crate. Nevertheless, these should have been foreseen or spotted early on by the **site supervisor**, so should not present problems immediately prior to the opening of the exhibition.

The press

If there is a press preview, it is often unofficially permissible (though most commercial exhibition rules forbid it in writing) for work to be completed while the press are around. It is forbidden because there are two sets of rules in public exhibition halls: one for when only the stand constructors and exhibitors are there, and another for when the press and public arrive. The most important rule applies to clear **gangways** for escape in case of fire, so if the work is continuing it can sometimes be got away with if it is low-profile and the gangway is kept clear of packaging or waiting exhibits. It is common practice, however, for many finishing touches to be applied at the feet of the journalists who turn up on **press day**.

Finally, the exhibition – be it trade fair stand or museum, gallery or heritage centre – is finished in every way. Exhibition staff are ready, in uniform or neatly dressed. The cleaners have clattered away, flicking off the last bits of dust as they left and everything is gleaming like a new pin. Everybody involved has had a good look round, checked every exhibit and read every label for misprints. The graphic designer has gone over every panel or label, touching out white specks with black and black with white, meticulously tidying where even the most sharp-eyed visitor will never look. The designer, smartly dressed and inwardly nervous, is outwardly calm and talks with one eye on a colleague and the other on the approach of a VIP or senior client.

The public

Then the public arrive. They take everything for granted, swooping and picking, homing in on the areas the designer hates and ignoring areas of gigantic effort.

The only place for the designer now is to be relaxing at home, with a big drink and a partner's sympathetic ear for the tribulations of the past weeks or months; a comforting presence as the exhausted genius worries darkly about whether the whole concoction will last the days, weeks, months or years for which it has been created.

Assessment

Sadly, this is not the end of the matter, for the best time to assess the successes or failures during production is quite soon after the opening. The job is fresh in the mind, the mistakes are clear and have not been rationalized out of existence, and the good aspects are immediately evident. A **post mortem** is not just the evaluation of the exhibition's qualities; it is the evaluation of production. With the client safely tucked up with the new acquisition it is a good time to take stock and highlight areas of misunderstanding and fail-ures in scheduling or delivery, or to discuss strengths and weaknesses in the production team. The best place for the post mortem is in a café near by the site, for the other impor-tant aspect is the immediate observation of visitor reaction, both to the specific exhibition stand and, almost equally importantly, the competition. A calm walk around an exhibition or trade fair with the colleagues involved in the production can be very rewarding. Objectivity is hard to come by after days of single-minded involvement, but an attempt at objective appraisal of the exhibition or stand and comparison of solutions will be invalu-able. Most trade fairs have a theme, therefore many designers will have been trying to solve similar problems of display, communication and construction. It will be well worth assessing these other solutions, for something can be learned from everything.

This kind of assessment is in fact the secret **portfolio** of a good designer. Sheer experience is an unbeatable commodity, and though the final chapter dwells on scientific attempts at objective appraisal, there is nothing so valuable to the designer as personal experience and observation.

While the on-site post mortem is of great value, it will be far too early to assess the real results of any particular enterprise. In a permanent exhibition the early post mortem will take place on or near the site, and the reasons for it are the same as for the tempo-rary exhibition. The real long-term assessment of the value of certain **treatments** and design approaches will emerge, when it is considered cost effective, from professional assessment of the results of the exhibition which are described in the final chapter.

On many permanent projects it is necessary finally to have a snagging or defects meeting immediately after the opening. Such a meeting will highlight minor failings in construction or materials and these will generally be put right by the contractor before the account is finally settled.

11 The maintenance

THERE is one solid fact about exhibitions: no technically sophisticated enterprise should be embarked upon without the certain knowledge that it can be maintained. There is an old maxim which says that there is nothing worse than a working exhibit that doesn't work. There are many worse things, actually, but old professionals like their old saws. Basically, do not start something which cannot be finished. This applies to anything that might be expected to fail or give trouble during a period of three days or more, and this of course includes lamps. Even the most simple illuminated display should be left with a small stock of replacement lamps when it is handed over to the client. If they are not all used, they would almost certainly have been needed if they were not there. This circumstance obviously ranges from simple lamp changing to the replacement of working parts in a sophisticated piece of technical equipment.

Access

The primary consideration is of course access. This can be gained to a display from nearly every direction, but it must be built in (see Chapter 6, p. 84). The best possible access, space provided, is from the rear. In a museum exhibition it is wise to allow a maintenance passage or alleyway all round the perimeter of the site. Thus, if the exhibition is intro-

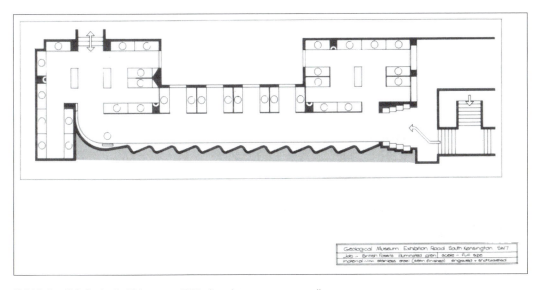

'British Fossils', Geological Museum, 1980. A maintenance access alley.

verted, within a room or hall, then a passageway at least 600 mm wide, accessible prefer-ably from outside the exhibition, should be provided.

This is naturally only a guide; introverted exhibitions come in many forms. If show-cases are back to back and there is no front access, often avoided for security reasons, then a spur to the access passage might run up between them both for maintenance and for **dressing**. If access has to be provided from the front, then a secure, preferably invis-ible method of locking must be used. There are many locks available, but certainly avoid anything with an exposed 'keyhole'. Little fingers (and sometimes big ones) stuff little things into keyholes. For some reason this is an irresistible temptation, the worst of which is chewing gum.

Overhead access can be given but it is frequently difficult, as with front access, to carry out essential maintenance during the open hours of the exhibition or museum. All these points apply equally to temporary exhibitions or stands; access must be considered, planned and built in. The best way to get it absolutely right is to consult with the techni-cians who will have to carry out the maintenance. Not only can they advise on access, but also on types of equipment which give less trouble than others. Some light fittings become infamous for the speed with which they consume lamps. All sorts of **projectors** have lamps, some better than others, some with automatic lamp-changing facilities. On really sophisticated setups, a unified maintenance facility is built in. In the US Pavilion at the Knoxville World Fair in Tennessee in 1982, a central control room not only contained all the video players required throughout the pavilion, but also monitored the failure of electronic devices in the building. The **Air and Space Museum** in Washington has the same facility. Both of these were new, purpose-built structures in which it is comparatively easy to build such services. At Disney World in Florida all the displays, restaurants and events are linked by an underground network of passages so that the whole campus can be serviced discreetly. In national museums in the UK and France, for instance, interference with the structure is frequently restricted by the inhibitions imposed by the 'listed' architecture, but there is no reason why – with attentive planning – good service facilities cannot be built in, in consultation with technicians and engineers.

Servicing and equipment

Temporary exhibitions are frequently serviced by the contractors or companies renting out the equipment. Flowers, for instance, which are by no means a technical exhibit but thought by some to enhance an exhibition stand, are hired out and maintained by their owners. The same is true of projection or moving image equipment, but if there are purpose-made special effects then ease of maintenance must be part of the brief in the first place and special arrangements must be made.

Water is generally considered a nightmare on any exhibition stand; not as a facility (normal plumbing can cope with that), but either as a decorative feature or as part of a technical exhibit. Pools and fountains can give a great deal of trouble if the plastic water-proofing is pierced accidentally (or deliberately), or if the pump fails. Water should only be used when it is essential to the display. If it is completely enclosed, then condensation will prove a problem unless forced ventilation is introduced. On a long-term exhibit, **fungicides** should be used in distilled water to avoid discoloration. Outdoors, water is far less trouble.

When considering A/V presentations, there are one or two factors that need attention. For permanent displays where slides are still used they will need replacing regularly, particularly if it is a non-stop display. It is best to have the display activated by the arrival of visitors, and this can be done either with pressure-pad switches beneath the carpeting, or ultrasonic or infra-red devices which sense the arrival of the visitor. If projection is the only way the pictures can be shown because of a large screen size or the demands of the physical circumstances, then stay with projection. If cost and circumstances permit, television monitors and multi-screen, plasma screen or flat screen presentations are worth thinking about with discs which are virtually indestructible; obviously everything used will eventually need servicing, but not nearly as rapidly as film. Again, these can be automatically activated but at the time of writing, cost for cost and considering maintenance problems, there are advantages to all methods depending on permanence and physical circumstances. The same is true of sound reproduction; solid state or discs are pretty well indestructable and present a real useful advance in technology.

When buying all types of equipment, the availability of spares must be considered. Brand new developments might be exciting, but when they rapidly out-date or are superseded, then spares become a problem. For a temporary exhibition, if a technical device is purchased then spares should be bought as part of the package, so that there will be no nasty surprises. It is rather like the good sense of taking vital car spares when motoring abroad.

There are some electronic or mechanical devices that are more stable and reliable than others; for instance, with slow revolves it is always wise to purchase a model that will bear a far heavier weight than actually required.

Running tungsten lamps at a lower voltage than that for which they are designed makes for a greatly lengthened life, but this is not possible with low voltage or fluorescent tubes. Television in all its forms needs less maintenance and is far more reliable than a sophisticated projector. There are always techniques which are more durable than others and therefore demand less attention. The competent designer must keep up to date with such things and ensure that the correct materials are specified. Ultraviolet is the great enemy of colour and fabrics under any circumstances. Filters can be applied to windows if direct sunlight is anywhere near to displays.

Security and surveillance

Security can present a problem for maintenance if there are valuable exhibits which also need proximate attention to equipment. Security guards have to be on hand while cases are opened and fittings changed. This is not because any of the maintenance crew are unreliable or dishonest, but because it is unfair to load the responsibility of security on to them. They are neither trained nor paid for it. Security or surveillance is the only real answer to vandalism which is rare in the countryside and provincial museums, but certainly quite common in national museums in large cities. It takes the form either of mindless assault – spraying sweet sticky substances such as Coca Cola, which is hard to remove, or bunging up holes with chewing gum or sweet papers – or concerted vandalism, when indelible felt-tip markers are deliberately taken into museums to damage artwork and fabric. Not only is vandalism more prevalent in inner-city areas, but it applies also, it seems, to boring or incomprehensible exhibits. This is in its own ghastly way understandable, if one thinks in terms of kicking in the television set (an inclination quite innocent people have had at one time or another).

Operating conditions

Another aspect of maintenance applies to equipment used to make life in an exhibition more bearable. This applies to fans, air-conditioning and **dust-proofing**. Again, it is a burden if not maintained adequately. Air-conditioning needs regular maintenance, and when showcases or areas of sensitive equipment are dust-proofed, the filters have to be changed regularly or the whole system becomes useless. This refers to showcases in which the exhibits are kept clean by pumping filtered air into them at a high enough pressure to keep the dirty air out. Obviously this is much more necessary in an urban atmosphere than in the cool, cleaner countryside. Again, this type of equipment, when used for short-term exhibitions, can be hired, so the maintenance can be hired along with it, daily or weekly checks being made by the contractor who has the **franchise** for that particular exhibition.

When changes of staff are necessitated for temporary or permanent exhibitions, it is important that the new staff should be fully briefed with regard to maintenance. To this end it is useful to have maintenance schedules and documents which are regularly updated for every contingency.

The final aspect of maintenance is simple cleaning. For temporary exhibitions at trade fairs, cleaning contractors exist and are generally franchised. They should attend daily before opening time to vacuum all floors, collect rubbish and dust showcases and exposed exhibits. This is standard practice, and when exhibition organizers publish their rules of attendance, such contractors are listed. In 'one-off' special exhibits, clearly special arrangements should be made.

Museums and galleries generally have either their own or contract cleaning staff to do the work. These again should be attended by security staff when necessary, but specialist cleaners should be employed where particular attention is necessary. The days of dusty, obscure museums ought to be over now that thoughtful direction and good design have been evident in UK museums since the 1960s.

Maintenance therefore is a job for professionals. They need to be consulted early, considered throughout and employed specifically. Whether they are contract or salaried, they are vital to the continued success of any exhibition. For portable or mobile exhibitions, employment must be considered at each venue, or the travelling display will suffer. Any final assessment of the success or failure of any exhibition must take into account its maintainability and the planning of any exhibition must learn from the successes or failures of previous ventures in this respect, as in any other.

12 The end result

WHAT, after all this is success? What is a good exhibition? Who decides whether it is good or not and what are the parameters it is judged by? There are too many questions and indeed not really enough answers.

A good exhibition in the simplest terms is one that patently achieves the aims it set out to achieve. But what are these aims? Are they simply to fulfil the brief when, as discussed earlier, the brief has probably – at least in part – been prepared by the designer? There has to be more to it than that. Also, since there are many different types of exhibition as described in Chapter 1, they must all be judged differently.

In the 12 or so years that have elapsed since the first edition of this book, considerable changes have taken place in the expectations of the public and the requirements for museum and heritage exhibitions. Governmental policies, shift of responsibility and emphasis have made demands on the public servants who ran the national museums that were generally beyond their capabilities to meet. Curators, conservators, academics and designers were steeped in an atmosphere of public service in which they were required to budget wisely but, more importantly, they were to serve the public with exhibitions and displays specifically designed to enlighten and inform (with a touch of delight thrown in where possible).

The museums were free of charge to enter and they had minimal ancillary services such as toilets, access for the disabled, cafés and shops. Nevertheless, between the mid-1960s and late 1980s they were presenting the public at best with some fine exhibitions. Also a pretty powerful influence had arrived in the UK from Canada and the US. In the early 1980s a travelling exhibition called 'Science Circus' had come to the Science Museum from the Ontario Science Centre. It was the first time that the British public, in an already popular museum, had been exposed to a really eclectic mix of what are now called **'hands-on'** exhibits: in other words, the extensive use of interactive displays to explain science and technology. The Science Museum capitalized on this and itself introduced the 'Launch Pad'. The direct interaction offered to the visitor in this exhibition, together with other similar permanent and travelling or temporary exhibitions around the country, radically changed the public's attitude to museums. It also persuaded designers and curators in many fields of the value of such exhibits in communicating with the public.

Thus great improvements had taken place, albeit in circumstances where visitor numbers were counted inaccurately; success was measured by observations of public reaction as well as praise or condemnation in the specialist press. (The national press only ever comment on content and very rarely on design.) Some few museums in the UK, the Natural History Museum for one, had set up units for visitor assessment. The original author of this chapter, Mic Alt – now sadly no longer with us – was the leader of that unit for a valuable period. The few national museums that did such work willingly shared their experience with other museums in the form of papers and lectures.

Then suddenly the world, for museums in the UK at least, turned upside down. Government funding was withdrawn or reduced. The buildings, once the property of a central agency, were handed over to the individual museums and a whole posse of commercially ignorant and innocent public servants were told to go out and bring paying visitors in to support their sometimes vast establishments. Thus, in a kind of controlled frenzy, a new breed of directors was born. Some were brought in from the commercial world, some had actual commercial savvy, and some were clever enough to employ the right assistance to lead them through the new territory in which they found themselves.

The world of commercial exhibitions has not really changed. Shows such as the Ideal Home Exhibition, the Motor Show or Boat Show have remained very much the same in style even if the techniques and materials have advanced. Trade fairs have always reflected the economy and conditions of their times, paradoxically some of the glossiest commercial exhibitions occurring in times of economic depression.

World fair design in the UK was affected by the closure or shrinkage imposed by new policies on some government departments. Where thinkers, writers and designers had been employed to put across an image of the country or government policy, suddenly they had all gone – some to freelance practices and others to early retirement. Experts drawn in from marketing, management, public relations and advertising companies were put in charge of the country's image. At the Class 1 World Fair in Seville in 1992 a pavilion was conceived and built without an initial reference to experienced exhibition designers and scriptwriters. The result, as mentioned earlier, was a pavilion completely useless for normal exhibition purposes.

Back in the national museums, in this frenzy of commercialism at which some were far better than others, exhibitions that might make money were conceived, designed by freelance practices, and built. The Natural History Museum, despite all other aspects of natural history, chose to focus on the ever-popular dinosaur and spine-chilled the public with animatronic orgies of prehistoric violence. Exhibitions appeared with titles such as 'Creepy-Crawlies', one not exactly designed to appeal to traditional museum visitors. Real artefacts became secondary to interpretations of reality based on contemporary science and designed to draw in the crowds of paying visitors. They did.

The National Lottery was introduced and drew large sums of money towards national and provincial institutions. One positively good thing was that funds from the Lottery were not available unless special consideration was given to the disabled. Large spaces previously devoted to the display of artefacts were now given over to restaurants and shops. Exhibitions were specifically designed with by-products in mind that would relate to the exhibitions but be available in the shops as souvenirs or toys. Whether academic standards were maintained, time alone will tell. In the author's view, some were chucked out of the window and some museums, galleries and heritage centres were conceived for entirely the wrong reasons. A business, of course, has to make money, but to allow the sponsors of an exhibition to dictate content, style, designer or architect is clearly wrong. Some museums, the Imperial War Museum for one, managed to achieve a fine balance. Some failed and others, such as the British Museum and a number of provincial museums, to their credit managed to survive without charging entrance fees.

Certain provincial museums and either local government or independent trusts leaped at the chance of Heritage Lottery funding for new or refurbished buildings and heritage centres. The wisest of these sought funding first for feasibility studies, as discussed in Chapter 3; others charged short-sightedly into enterprises that were more designed to reflect the status of the organizers than to satisfy a public need. Very few enterprises were embarked upon with a clear overall view of what the public might respond to, might really derive something from, and might return to again and again.

Along with government policies the public had also changed. Stimulated by advertising and such high profile enterprises as Jorvik, The White Cliffs Experience and Wigan Pier, everything now was an *experience*. Leisure was no longer sitting down with a good book by the fire; it now had to be organized. The word 'experience' was so over-used that those in the business rapidly came to wince at its very mention. The term 'heritage' too had become devalued by rapidly and thoughtlessly erected edifices or experiences that contained in reality nothing worthwhile. But the British public, probably not at all uniquely, made very few demands. It simply stayed away if it did not like something and went if it did.

Now, with shopping experiences like the Trafford Centre in Manchester, Lakeside at Thurrock and others dotted around the country, the public actually regards shopping as a leisure activity or hobby. The Natural History Museum has observed this fact and the whole of the new set of exhibitions in the Earth Sciences wing looks far more like a shopping experience than a museum; indeed, where there once was a small shop there is now a large information desk; where there once was a major exhibition there is now a huge shop. The exhibitions themselves contain a profusion of faults that the previous generation of designers had learnt to avoid: type that is too small, poorly-lit labels, headings out of sight above the visitor's head, arrows to direct the visitor around and so on.

The Trafford Centre in Manchester is a totally commercial venture. Among an appealing if Rabelaisian jungle of styles and themes, a 1980s Mercedes coupé is railed off as an exhibit. A label describes it as belonging to the wife of the businessman who conceived and masterminded the enterprise. Is it an exhibit, a memorial to her or a signal that, with hard work and business acumen, you too can give your wife an expensive car?

Perhaps we will all eventually become de-confused and, in the nature of all fashions, a different reality will emerge. If it does, it can only do so with the help of sincere motives and proper evaluation, not only of the public's superficial desires but also more importantly of their needs on a broader scale. There is surely a requirement for any public in any civilized society to be well informed, aware of its history and origins and productively critical of its surroundings. There is, therefore, a need for the curators of our heritage to think ahead of the public and give them not only what they want, but what it might be benefi-cial for them to have.

What has all this got to do with the exhibition designer? A great deal. Designers too should avoid deceiving the public or condescending to the lowest common denominator in society in any area of exhibition design, especially if he or she cares about the role of design in society, and most particularly the role of exhibition design in *informing* society.

There is a truth in exhibitions: the real thing is there, be it a car or boat for eventual sale, real dinosaur bones, a fossil or ancient artefact. If we replace the truth with repre-sentations of the truth, then an exhibition is no more valuable than a television set.

As a result of all the changes mentioned above, a great deal of design work became available. Design practices sprang up almost from nowhere. Architects leaped at exhibi-tion design; large design companies known for graphics, 3-D, packaging or interiors suddenly added exhibitions to their list of capabilities. The mistakes and bad judgements that had slowly been disappearing from the discipline in the 1970s and 1980s started to reappear. Obviously there were and continue to be some fine exhibition designers and design practices, but a huge number of new ones sprang into being, not even aware in many cases that experienced designers already existed. They started with enormous zeal to re-invent the wheel. They were of course constrained by the need to survive, to pay their staff and partners, to get more work no matter what. Research went out of the window.

In the large organizations that had employed design teams to do their exhibition work there had been time for experiment, for a body of experience and knowledge to build up. Suddenly that was all lost. There was no longer time to learn lessons from what had gone before. The only areas in which real innovations took place were in materials and tech-nology such as A/V, **virtual reality** and computing. Other traditional but very effective techniques were being forgotten about or ignored.

Techniques were being used because they were fashionable in their own right, not because they were the best way of telling a particular story. Style and fashion became the order of the day; nobody was examining whether it really worked on many fronts any more. Provided it paid, it worked. In the marketing jargon of the 1990s, 'it washed its face', in other words the money it pulled in paid for its production and upkeep.

Times perhaps are changing. The types of evaluation Mic Alt wrote about are being examined again: so what are they?

Formative evaluation

As soon as the designer makes an attempt to implement the agreed strategy, steps can be taken to **evaluate** the success with which the implementation is proceeding. These eval-uations are aimed at shaping the form of the final product. The evaluator will usually carry out research on '**mock-up**' displays to check whether they are achieving the desired reactions from visitors. Feedback will thus be gained on how the displays are working and what effect they are having.

Consumer reactions have to be interpreted with considerable sensitivity to stimulate the creative process further and to ensure that good ideas are not killed simply because they were not properly presented in mock-up form.

Evaluations using mock-ups are usually conducted among small samples representative of the target audience in an open-ended and qualitative fashion, since the main emphasis is on discovering how the content might be better represented. The strength of an effective rational argument is more likely to be apparent despite crude presentation, as arguments depend on logically and psychologically-constructed prose as well as typography and graphics. It is clear that evaluations of a mock-up will not indicate a great deal about the emotional appeal of a display as it would appear in a real exhibition.

The outcome of these early evaluations will typically take the form of discussions between the evaluator, the writer or initiator of the information and the designer in which proposals for remedying any weak points in the communications will be put forward.

Objective evaluation

Before an exhibition is built it is generally necessary to obtain **approval** from the client. Often the designer will have produced a three-dimensional model or visual of the exhibition, together with a detailed specification of the products/artefacts to be included as well as the accompanying text and graphics. It is at this stage that final approval for the designs is sought. The evaluator's role is to produce the objective evidence that has been collected which justifies the proposed design solutions. The evaluator will help provide reassurances on how and why the particular exhibition will work among its intended audience. (Objectivity is not that easy to come by; every assessment made is in part influenced by the evaluator's own personality and ability to communicate. To be of any real use in these circumstances the evaluator must have the respect of the client.)

Summative evaluation

After the exhibition has opened, the evaluator will be concerned with discovering the impact of the exhibition upon its visitors. Among other things, he will be interested in establishing the extent to which the objectives or aims of the exhibition have been met and whether the exhibition can be improved upon in any way, and if so, how. This will not apply to short-term exhibitions.

Perhaps the major purpose in evaluating an exhibition after it is opened to the public is that it provides the evaluators, and through them the design and production team, with the opportunity of learning from their mistakes. The information thus collected should be assimilated by the design team so that they can avoid making similar mistakes in the future.

However, Dr Patricia Sterry, Director of Heritage Design Studies at the University of Salford, says that there is a real challenge in integrating visitor studies with the heritage design process, and her thorough analysis provides several reasons for this. She maintains that most designers are unaware that such information is available. There is difficulty in knowing where to get information due to its lack of availability. Even if designers can obtain visitor study information, she says, it is unreadable; the language is often too technical and not geared towards the sort of information that designers would want. Designers often assimilate information far better by observation rather than by reading or instruction. Dr Sterry's thesis is that there is no widespread interest or support for using or commissioning such information among designers. She says that there are no strategies or guidelines for studies that are (or seem) particularly relevant to designers, and that visitor study programmes are costly to undertake and are extremely time consuming.

The fact that we, as designers, choose to ignore that there is either a body of information on the nature of visitors, or indeed that we could find out more about those who benefit from the things we design but do not, is pretty damning.

It is worth discussing, however, the confusion referred to earlier in some depth. We in the UK are becoming either gadget-obsessed or nostalgia-obsessed. As to the former, having run out of any real necessities as a society, we are buying things that we might one day need and simply please us. In the last centuries as far as ergonomics are concerned, design has moved in where evolution has left off. Tools which had evolved to be sublimely practical became obsolete with the discovery of various alternative forms of power. Man and horse were replaced by water, which was replaced by steam, and then oil. Tools today are designed both to function and to sell. Either is likely to satisfy the manufacturer, as long as it sells. Often, as is the case with some items of furniture, the 'sitting' tool is bought only for its looks. There is a danger that exhibitions might go the same way and some already have. Those that are conceived and presented for funding in order to perform a public service in museums and heritage centres, as well as some experiences, are in danger of being deemed successful simply because they are pleasing. They are so attention-grabbing that they get the required numbers of visitors through their doors to pay their way; therefore they are successful. The fact that nobody is in the least bit enlightened by them goes unnoticed.

Landmark architecture comes in to the same category. A building may be so striking that it attracts crowds of people in its own right. This may gratify the architect, the commissioners of the building, and those involved who are looking for honours or prizes. But if it is designed for a purpose and does not function satisfactorily as such, it must be a failure. The paradox is that some buildings are designed before their purpose is properly defined. Even worse, some buildings are built before the function is clear. The sad thing is that even bad buildings can be so sculpturally attractive that they work marvellously as commercial ventures. They are in fact just like a cripplingly uncomfortable Starck chair: beautiful but useless – the dumb blondes of the design world.

Nostalgia obsession is quite different and is generally to be found in the generation of an age above 55, people known in marketing jargon as empty-nesters (their mortgage is paid off and the children have left home). Perhaps put off in their youth by dull visits to boringly-presented and élitist collections, the word 'museum' conjures up for them a poor image. The term 'heritage' carries no such baggage and has become acceptable, so that in the last 10 to 15 years heritage centres have proliferated around the UK (though often their title disguises the fact that they are, in reality, museums). The research conducted into heritage centre visitation and design by Dr Sterry makes very compelling reading. Put quite simply, late middle-aged 'working class' folk (C2s, Ds and Es in marketing jargon) with the time and the money enjoy going to old buildings, where they can reminisce with each other over bits and pieces associated with their early lives. They are not, as with more educated or well-read visitors (As, Bs and C1s), interested in ancient history or even comparatively recent history; only their own remembered history. This is particularly true of heritage centres where pride in the community is generated by recapturing the youth of the local inhabitants. Such sentimental journeys are, however, of little interest to visitors from well outside the area.

The fear of the author and others is that both commissioners of work and designers themselves will be over-influenced by those responsible for marketing. They will continually exploit these two obsessions, so that they end up by condescending to the public and obliterating the truth that is inherent in the display of actual objects. Exhibition design is a modern, poorly understood and barely recognized design discipline. It is far too important to the national economy, enlightenment and educational standards to be reduced to the level of advertising.

Experts in evaluation and marketing must work with the commissioners and designers to maintain the integrity of the profession and the quality of the end result. Professional exhibition designers should therefore embrace wholeheartedly the need for all kinds of evaluation, and encourage their clients to do the same. The more designers who do so, the better respected the profession will become, the better exhibition designs will emerge and the better the world will be.

Bibliography

Allwood, J. (1977), *The Great Exhibitions*, London: Studio Vista.

Belcher, M. (1991), *Exhibitions in Museums*, Leicester: Leicester University Press.

Black, M. (ed.) (1950), *Exhibition Design*, London: Architectural Press.

Earnscliffe, J. (1992), *In Through the Front Door – Disabled People and the Visual Arts*, London: Arts Council of Great Britain.

Gardner, J. and Heller, C. (1960), *Exhibitions and Display*, London: Batsford.

Gill, J. (1997), *Access Prohibited? Information for Designers of Public Access Terminals*, London: RNIB.

Goldsmith, S. (1976), *Designing for the Disabled*, London: RIBA Publications.

Gregory, W. (1996), *The Informability Manual*, London: HMSO.

Hall, M. (1987), *On Display: a design grammar for museum exhibitions*, London: Lund Humphries.

Harrison, R. (ed.) (1994), *Heritage Management*, London: Butterworth Heinemann.

Johnson, N. (1984), 'Visitors with a Physical Handicap', *Museums Journal*, 84 (1), p. 36, London.

Matthews, G. (1990), *Museums and Art Galleries*, London: Butterworth Architecture.

Nolan, G. (1997), *Designing Exhibitions to include People with Disabilities: a Practical Guide*, Edinburgh: National Museums of Scotland.

Ryan, D.S. (1997), *The Ideal Home Through the 20th Century*, London: Hazar Publishing.

Screven, C. (1974), *The Measurement and Facilitation of Learning in the Museum Environment: an Experimental Analysis*, Washington: Smithsonian Institution.

Screven, C. (1976), *Exhibit Evaluation: A Goal-referenced Approach*, Washington: Curator.

Simpson, R. (1997), *Videowalls*, London: Focal Press.

Sixsmith, M. (ed.) (1995), *Touring Exhibitions*, London: Butterworth Heinemann.

Sparke, P. (ed.) (1986), *Did Britain Make It?*, London: Design Council.

Spencer, H. and Reynolds, L. (1977), *Directional Signing and Labelling in Libraries and Museums: a review of current theory and practice*, London: Royal College of Art.

Thompson, J.M.A. (ed.) (1984), *Manual of Curatorship: a guide to museum practice*, London: Butterworth Heinemann/The Museums Association.

Vergo, P. (ed.) (1988), *The New Museology,* London: Reaktion Books.

Glossary

All the terms in this glossary have been highlighted in **bold** at their first appearance.

Acrylic A thermoplastic of the same type as Perspex or Plexiglass, usually transparent.

Air and Space The name for various museums, particularly the one in Washington DC, part of the Smithsonian.

Aisle The space between lines of exhibition stands. The central or main passage between exhibits.

Ambient light The actual, overall light level of an exhibition environment.

Animation The art of making animated cartoon films; hence the term 'animated film' for a serious production.

Animated model A model of a person or animal which moves, simulating reality.

Animatronics Mechanically-animated humans or animals, often associated with a sound track.

Approval The stage at which a client's final agreement to a design scheme is given.

Artefacts Old or new man-made objects.

Artist's impression A drawing done by a designer to give an impression of how an exhibition (or building) will look on completion.

Artwork The original material prepared by an illustrator or graphic designer for reproducing on to display panels.

A/V Audio-visual; an effect using both sound and vision, generally slide shows, television screens or projections.

Backdrop A flat painted, coloured or photographed screen or scene behind a display to give an illusion of place or space.

Back-lit Lit from the back, particularly a transparent photograph.

Bold A heavy, big-bodied typeface.

Books-on-legs A derogatory name for any display or exhibition with too many words.

Booth A small stall or partially enclosed shell scheme stand at a trade fair.

Brief A concise synopsis of the requirements.

Budget The actual financial allocation to any particular project.

Buried loop A transmitting circuit built into an exhibition to carry an audio commentary.

By-laws Local regulations which control structures, aisle widths and opening hours of exhibitions and particularly fire precautions.

CAD Computer Aided Design.

Caption A larger, more general version of a label.

Chiaroscuro The management and effect of light and shade.

Commentary The recorded, spoken accompaniment to a display, A/V programme or sequence of special effects.

Commercial Attaché the member of an embassy staff in charge of trade or business affairs.

Concept study A study to examine the type of design most likely to solve a problem.

Condensed A narrow, close-packed typeface.

Conduiting Tubing or ducting, in metal or plastic, usually used to carry electrical services.

Conferences Large business or professional gatherings, in this context usually associated with exhibitions.

Conservation The science of preserving our heritage; hence conservator: a specialist in a field of conservation.

Context The subject range of an exhibition.

Contract The legally binding arrangement as to cost and time between a contractor and the client.

Copywriter One who writes text for exhibitions or programmes.

Cornice A decorative detail or moulding between walls and ceiling to effect a neat joint or give an impression of greater height or width.

Counter As in a shop, used by receptionists or stand staff to dispense literature and so on.

Craftsperson A skilled, trained maker of things; a carpenter, painter or modeller.

Credentials pitch A demonstration of a designer's past successes and ability to do the job.

Credit An acknowledgement of a person's or company's contribution to a production, usually on a Credit Panel in a prominent part of an exhibition.

Cross-fade To change a projected still picture by fading down from one and up on the other, using two projectors on to the same screen.

Curator A person in charge of a museum or objects in a museum. Usually the source of information for a museum exhibition.

Cut-away A man-made object with a piece removed neatly to expose its workings.

Cut-away diagram A drawing to explain any object representing part of the object removed to expose the inside.

Cut-out lettering Lettering made by cutting out sheet material to the shape of letters or logos.

Detail A small, intimate piece of design, drawn at full size; hence detail drawing.

Diorama A three-dimensional display, part-model, part-painting. A working diorama: one with moving parts or lighting to simulate activity.

Disc (or disk) A computer disc containing pictorial or audio information as stills, or moving images with a sound track.

Double-decker An exhibition stand or construction composed of two decks or two or more floors.

Double-sided A display panel, case or area that can be seen from each side.

Draughtsperson A specialist in drawing up designs.

Drawing board A smooth, flat board on which drawings are prepared, usually with precision horizontal and vertical line drawing instruments.

Dressing The art of displaying objects in a showcase attractively and effectively.

Duodecimal The system of measurement using 12 parts to a measure, for example 12″ to 1′0″. A foot is technically obsolete in the UK but is still commonly used. It remains in use in the US.

Dust-proof A sealed case or showcase. A case into which filtered air is pushed out faster than unfiltered air can drift in.

Ecocentre A public place devoted to exhibitions of local ecology and its interpretation. It is most common in France.

Edge lighting The effect caused by light travelling laterally across Perspex or glass sheeting and being emitted at the edge or where the sheet is engraved, using clear, coloured or fluorescent Perspex.

Electronics The technology of the use of electrical systems for special effects and display devices.

Elevation A drawing done to scale of the side view of an exhibition.

Entertainment space Private or secluded space set aside for the entertainment of important visitors; hospitality suite.

Estimate The carefully calculated cost of a piece of construction; often produced in competition with other contractors.

Evaluation The science of assessing the worth or usefulness of something. Testing an exhibition's possibilities of success beforehand. Assessing reaction during, and summarizing the results afterwards.

Exhibition A fair, show, display, expo or any display of objects for select or public view.

Exhibition contractor Company or individual specializing in building exhibitions.

Exhibition space Part of an exhibition set aside for display.

Exhibitor A company or company's representative initiating or taking part in an exhibition or trade fair.

Experience An event which physically involves the visitor – a ride, for instance.

External lighting Light coming from outside an exhibition or display case.

Extra Any item not included in the original drawings or estimates and therefore executed on site.

Extrovert exhibition One designed to be approached or appreciated from the outside, on an island or near-island site.

Eye level The height of the eye relative to the display. For general purposes, approximately 1600 mm above floor level for adults. Special allowances should be made for children and the disabled.

Fade To lower lighting levels. See also cross-fade.

Fair An exhibition, display or show of goods and objects for commercial reasons. A world fair or trade fair.

Fascia board The board at the front or leading edges of an exhibition to carry titles, names and so on.

Feasibility study A study designed to examine the feasibility of a proposed project.

Fibre optics Flexible glass or plastic fibres used to carry light for great distances. Either optically correct or for illumination only.

Film loop A continuous loop of film giving repeated showings of the same sequence.

Fire resistant Will not immediately catch fire, but will eventually.

Flat display Text and pictures only.

Flight simulator A complex device to train pilots using a mock-up cockpit and models and videos of airports, landscapes and flight situations.

Flip-over panels A solid or hard paged book on a large scale.

Fluorescent Substances which glow when an electric current is passed through them, or a powerful light is shone on them.

Franchise A special arrangement whereby a contractor, or a selected group of contractors, can supply services to a trade fair or major exhibition.

Fret-cut Holes cut out of a solid sheet.

Fungicide A chemical used to kill fungi which might otherwise colour or spoil water displays.

Gallery An art gallery. A part of a major museum. A raised walkway.

Gangway The aisle or space between exhibits at a trade fair.

Geodesic dome A light, strong structure made by combining a grid of triangular elements formed from rods and fabrics.

Geological reserve A large area of outstanding geological interest, usually with interpretative exhibitions at the centre or sites of special interest.

Ghost An image produced by projection on gauze or screen material.

Ghoster All night work on an exhibition; 'doing a ghoster'.

Glass painting Paintings on the back of one or more layers of glass or clear Perspex giving at best a deep, luminescent image.

Graphics Flat two-dimensional treatment of images and text.

GRP Glass reinforced plastic. A plastic or resin made and formed cold, and reinforced with glass fibres.

Halogen An element which, alone or in conjunction with quartz, produces a hot powerful light when electricity is passed through it.

Handrail A safety rail on a staircase or balcony, or a rail to keep the public at a distance from the exhibits.

Handset As on a telephone. A method of communicating a commentary without disturbing other visitors.

Hands-on A phrase used to describe exhibits which can be handled or operated.

Headroom Space beneath overhead structure to allow for easy movement and circulation.

Heritage centre A place for the exhibition and interpretation of the local built environment.

Hologram An image made photographically, with laser light, to give an impression of three dimensions.

Imagineering A word invented by the Disney Corporation for the creativity involved in animatronics.

Imax A film and projection system using 70 mm film stock and special sound effects to create a powerful impression of real movement on a massive, close screen.

Indemnity A type of insurance or guarantee made by the government to cover the cost of loss or damage.

Industrial shed A prefabricated structure made for factory use.

Inflatable Any structure made with inflatable bars joined by fabric or a structure with sealed doors kept up by constant pressure.

Information only A text-only display – a 'book-on-legs'.

Informative display Simply to inform.

Infra-red Invisible light used to activate proximity switches and so on.

Interactive A type of display which responds to the visitor's input.

Interpreting The word used to describe the activity of designers and writers simplifying complex information produced by specialists, for easy comprehension by ordinary people.

Introvert exhibition One designed to be appreciated entirely from within, in an enclosed space.

Island site An exhibition site with no immediate neighbours; isolated by aisles or gangways.

Italic A sloping typeface.

Keyboard A matrix of buttons with numbers, letters or symbols giving access to a computer-controlled display.

Label The short text and its 'card' directly concerning an exhibit. Its title, size, provenance, code number and so on.

Laser A narrow, intense and accurate beam of light used to make holograms or dramatic lighting effects.

Layout A plan showing the positions of parts of the story, exhibits and displays.

Light A slim, delicately wrought typeface.

Light-box A white or silvered box with an opal top and fluorescent lights used to back-light photographs, transparencies or slides.

Linear lighting Lighting along a line or set of lines, or behind a cornice or skirting, to give effects of distance, division or space.

Literature Reading material freely available in an exhibition.

Logo An identifying symbol consisting of a simple picture or design and/or letters.

Loop absorber A box of spools used to contain, in a compact form, a loop of cine film.

Maintenance The support required for electrical or special effects of one kind or another.

Management A vital part of the production process: its organization.

Massing The positioning of solid or semi-solid objects relative to each other.

Mechanical engineering The technology required for the design and manufacture of special effects and display devices of one sort or another.

Medium (1) A typeface between light and bold in weight.

Medium (2) The selected means of communication.

Mock-up A full-size model of a display, clearly temporary, used for evaluating a display's potential or workability.

Model An accurate small-scale representation in three dimensions.

Moiré A watery pattern from watered silk or mohair. A pattern arising from one set of lines passing in front of another.

Multi-screen An audio-visual presentation of slides or television on more than one screen.

Mural A large painting, photograph or photomontage. A representational wall covering.

Narrative The story or theme of an exhibition.

Negative The transparent, reversed film image from which a print is made.

Neon A gas which glows red when charged with an electric current. Gives its name to various gases in bent glass tubes, giving off bright coloured light.

One-off A single purpose-made exhibit or device.

Opal Semi-translucent white glass or plastic used between the source of light and a transparency.

Open day A day upon which an establishment is thrown open to the public.

Panel The name for part of a wall in an exhibition, normally of light construction and non-load bearing, measuring 2.4 × 1.2 × 0.05 m. A display panel: one carrying graphic material.

Partition The normal name for an exhibition wall made up from stock panels as above.

Pavilion A special, generally temporary building erected to contain a national exhibition at a world or trade fair.

Pepper's Ghost A device for replacing one three-dimensional image gradually with another in the same place.

Perspective A drawing done by a designer or on a computer to give an impression of how an exhibition will look on completion.

Perspex A form of thermoplastic of extreme clarity used in place of glass.

Plastic laminate Opaque, hard, durable, variously coloured and textured surface.

Platform A wooden plinth, usually 100 mm high, upon which large commercial exhibition stands are built.

Polaroid© Light polarizing material used for animated diagrams.

Portfolio The book or folder of photographs of work by a designer or design firm.

Post mortem An examination of the problems that arose during production.

Pre-project A French phrase for early planning stages.

Presentation A word sometimes used to describe a display. The showing of a scheme to a client.

Press day The day immediately before an exhibition opens, set aside for visiting journalists.

Pressure pad A switch set beneath a carpet to activate a display on the visitor's arrival.

Production chart A diagram produced by hand or computer to define production stages or phases.

Production Manager Actually supervises the production, a great deal of the time on site.

Production schedule The listed deadline dates for all phases of production.

Program The specific set of instructions and responses inserted into a computer.

Programme A timed sequence of sounds and/or pictures to convey a story or message.

Project manager The manager appointed for one particular project.

Projector A device for projecting a sharp, focused image, either still or moving.

Prototype A working model of a proposal or project – a 'one-off'.

Public space Areas allocated for the use or passage of the public.

Pulsed tape A tape emitting signals to initiate activities or effects.

Purpose made Made for that exact purpose only, one-off.

Quartz A silicon mineral which, in conjunction with other elements and electricity, produces a bright light.

Radar Radio signals, the interruption of which can activate a switch.

Radio Short wave or buried loop. A means of communicating within an exhibition to individual visitors in specific areas.

Random access Swift access to pictures and/or text via projectors or disc players, facilitated by a computer.

Recessive A style of design presentation wherein the objects on display totally dominate the design treatment.

Replica An apparently exact reproduction of anything from a jewel to a steam engine.

Representative (Rep) Generally a sales person present on a commercial exhibition stand and essential to its function.

Reproduction The general name for the many methods of copying pictures and text for display purposes.

Revolves Continuous or pulsed turntables of any size.

Rods A term sometimes used for 'setting out' drawings.

Rotagraphics® A patented device for changing a picture or sign three times within the same flat plane. See also Toblerone.

Rotosign© A patented device for producing many back- or front-lit pictures within the same flat area.

Running titles Titles that run continuously through an exhibition.

Scale The comparative measurements used for drawings smaller than the real thing.

Science centre A museum or exhibition centre devoted to explaining science by example and interaction.

Screen printing A method of printing using photographically produced stencils on a silk screen.

Screens White or silvered, solid or translucent surfaces to receive projection. Divisions between one area and another.

Scriptwriter A specialist in producing researched text for an exhibition or commentary.

Section A drawing showing what an exhibition, display or detail might look like if cut straight through. An explanatory drawing.

Semi-silvered glass Literally glass half-obscured by silvering, used for making Pepper's Ghosts.

Setting out Producing drawings at full size from scale drawings for the use of the craftsman.

Shell scheme A layout of booths or stalls for a trade fair providing walls, fascias, lighting and minimal floor covering.

Shopfitter A company specializing in building shop fronts and interiors, and sometimes exhibitions.

Signing off Acquiring a signature of approval from the initiator of a piece of text or diagram.

Simplified keyboard A limited number of buttons giving access to a computer-controlled display.

Site The actual geographical location of an exhibition or its position within a trade fair.

Site supervisor A specialist who supervises all the construction work on the exhibition site.

Skirting A space between walls and floor protected by being recessed or covered in durable material.

Snagging Going over a job immediately after completion to eliminate all problems or snags.

Solid state Computers, sound or pictures contained in a device with no moving parts.

Special effects Any electronic, mechanical (or both) device for communicating or enhancing a display.

Specification A document describing exactly the work to be done.

Split screen One screen on to which are projected several different but associated images.

Sprawling project A project which has evolved to be huge and complex beyond the original concept.

Square metre super A square metre of floor space extended upwards to the top of the structure.

Stall A small booth or enclosure at a trade fair or market.

Stand The usual name for an exhibition construction at a trade fair or special exhibition.

Stencil A method of printing where ink or paint is pushed through an outline to leave a precise shape.

Story line The main gist or theme of an exhibition or programme.

Stripping off The removal of all protective coverings from an exhibition immediately prior to opening.

Synopsis A brief, concise description of the requirements of an exhibition.

System A prefabricated exhibition construction kit.

Systematic A manner of displaying information in an ordered way, using relative factors found within the subject.

Tableaux Life-size presentations using models, artefacts and clothes to re-create a possible scene of bygone years or contemporary life.

'Talking Head'© A talking face projected on to a white relief model which, with a sound track, gives the illusion of a real person talking.

Television monitor A special television set specifically for viewing type, disc or computer-generated information.

Tender An estimate document, usually competitive; another word for estimate.

Thematic A way of ordering an exhibition based on a narrative.

Thermoplastic A plastic made and formed using heat.

Tier A level in a hierarchic display. A seating level.

Tilt A tilting mechanism.

Toblerone® A Swiss chocolate bar, equilaterally triangular in section, giving its name to any part of a display device that resembles it. See also Rotagraphics®.

Trade fair An exhibition, display or show of goods or objects for commercial exposition.

Transparency A transparent photograph which has to be viewed on or with a light-box.

Treatment A concise description of the method of presenting information using illustrations, objects and text.

TTS True to scale. A drawing done to scale which can be measured off using a scale rule.

Tug A heavy duty vehicle used for towing caravans carrying mobile exhibitions.

Tungsten An element which glows white hot when an electrical current is passed through it.

Typeface The style, form and detailed shape of lettering; each different one named.

Typography The art or style of printing.

Ultrasonic A method of remote control.

Ultraviolet Invisible light, damaging to coloured materials and photographs but useful for stimulating U/V sensitive materials to produce irridescent effects; black light.

Unplaned Raw, sawn timber from the cutting mill.

Venue The common name for the place at which an exhibition is held.

Vertical space Space devoted to display, communication and circulation control.

Viewing angle The angle from which a display is best seen.

Virgin client A client who has never commissioned an exhibition, museum or gallery before.

Virtual reality A 3D-simulation of actuality – a flight simulator, for instance.

Visual A drawing done by a designer or computer to give an impression of how an exhibition will look on completion.

Voids Dead areas where too many objects of minor interest are placed together, or none at all.

Wall In the exhibition context, usually plywood or hardboard on framing, or chipboard or some other patent board. Never load-bearing.

Working drawing A drawing done by a designer or draughtsperson for a builder to work from.

Working model Same as an animated model. Usually applies to small-scale replicas which work or operate like the real thing.

Workshop The place of work or factory of craftspeople or contractors.

World fair An exposition of the achievements of many countries in national pavilions.

Yellow Pages A directory of companies and business listed under professional, trade or craft names.

Index

Page references to figures appear in italics.

Picture credits

p. xvi: Design Council/Interieur; p. 1: Godbold Advertising; p. 2: Angex Ltd; p. 3: Britain on View BTA/ETB; p. 4: top, COI, bottom, NEC; p. 5: NEC; p. 6: top, NEC, bottom, Business Design Centre; p. 7: Furneaux Stewart and Spectrum Communications/Nicholas Gentilli; p. 8: Giles Velarde; p. 9: COI; p. 10: top, COI, bottom, Rex Features/Trippett SIPA Press; p. 12: top, British Marine Federation Industries, bottom, Harry Smith Collection; p. 13: Universal Pictorial Press; p. 14: Government of Ontario, Canada; p. 15: top, James Gardner/3D Concepts Ltd, bottom, Musée Camarguais; p. 16: British Museum; p. 17: Design Council; p. 18: top, Geological Museum, bottom left and bottom right, Design Council; p. 19: Hayward Gallery, South Bank Centre; p. 20: left, York Archaeological Trust, right, COI; p. 21: COI; p. 22: left, Design Council/Click Systems, right, Rex Features/Trippett SIPA Press; p. 23: York Archaeological Trust; p. 24: National Motor Museum, Beaulieu; p. 25: Giles Velarde; p. 27: Mary Evans Picture Library; p. 28: Donald Cooper/Photostage; p. 31: Furneaux Stewart and Visage Productions; p. 32: Design Council; p. 33: left, Honeywell Equipment Ltd, right, Adrian Wood; p. 34: Design Council; p. 35: Design Council/Guinness; p. 38: Geological Museum; p. 39: Giles Velarde; p. 40: Giles Velarde; p. 49: top and bottom, Giles Velarde; p. 51: British Museum; p. 53: Geological Museum; p. 56: Giles Velarde; p. 58: Design Council; p. 62: Sun Newspapers Ltd; p. 63: Giles Velarde; p. 65: Design Council; p. 66: Design Council; p. 67: Tate Gallery/David Clarke; p. 69: RSPB; p. 72: Monotype Corporation plc; p. 73: left and right, COI; p. 74: top and bottom, Wood & Wood International Signs; p. 75: Design Council; p. 76: Design Council; p. 77: top and bottom, Giles Velarde; p. 79: left, Susan Trangmar, right, Derek Pratt; p. 80: COI; p. 81: V&A Picture Library; p. 84: Giles Velarde; p. 86: Giles Velarde; p. 87: The National Gallery; p. 88: Land Design Studio; p. 90: Mary Evans Picture Library; p. 92: Design Council/Ian Dobbie; p. 93: COI; p. 94: COI; p. 95: Design Council; p. 96: top, Design Council, bottom, Sainsbury Archive; p. 99: Design Council; p. 100: top, Tri-Sign by Standeasy Display Systems Ltd, bottom, Marler Haley Exposystems Ltd; p. 101: Furneaux Stewart and Porsche Cars, Great Britain/Nicholas Gentilli; p. 102: Design Council; p. 103: left, Design Council, right, George Philip & Son Ltd; p. 104: Design Council/Ian Dobbie; p. 105: Land Design Studio; p. 110: V&A Picture Library; p. 111: top, Museum of London, bottom, Design Council; p. 112: top and bottom, Kandor Modelmakers Ltd; p. 114: Technical Animations Ltd; p. 115: Holographics (UK) Ltd/Andy Atkinson; p. 117: Design Council; p. 120: Design Council/Richard Waite; p. 121: I Laser Sound + Vision Ltd/Andy Atkinson; p. 122: Furneaux Stewart; p. 123: Design Council/Ian Dobbie; p. 124: York Archaeological Trust; p. 129: left, Design Council/Ian Dobbie, right, Design Council; p. 133: Land Design Studio; p. 134: Land Design Studio; p. 135: Furneaux Stewart and Seat Concessionaires UK Ltd/Nicholas Gentilli; p. 139: C-Beck Ltd; p. 141: Rediffusion Simulation Ltd; p. 142: Rediffusion Simulation Ltd; p. 151: COI; p. 159: Geological Museum. All sketches are by the author.